Reclaiming My Pride

RECLAIMING MY PRIDE

FROM TRAGEDY TO TRIUMPH

How I Took Over My Husband's Car Dealerships and Steered My Way to a New Life

SUZANNE IOVANNA

RECLAIMING MY PRIDE
*From Tragedy to Triumph. How I Took over My Husband's
Car Dealerships and Steered My Way to a New Life*

FIRST EDITION

ISBN   978-1-5445-5017-6   *Hardcover*
       978-1-5445-5016-9   *Paperback*
       978-1-5445-5018-3   *Ebook*

CONTENTS

INTRODUCTION 9

OCTOBER 19, 2014 11

PART I: BEFORE

1. SUZANNE, GIRL 19

2. SUZANNE, TEEN 29

3. SUZANNE, WORKING GIRL 35

4. SUZANNE, GIRLFRIEND... 39

5. SUZANNE, WIFE AND MOTHER.. 47

PART II: AFTER

6. SUZANNE, WIDOW 65

7. SUZANNE, DETECTIVE 75

8. SUZANNE, DEFENDANT 83

9. SUZANNE, RECRUIT 95

10. SUZANNE, CHANGEMAKER 105

11. SUZANNE, DEALMAKER 117

12. SUZANNE, STUDENT 127

13. SUZANNE, GIRLFRIEND 2.0...................................... 137

14. SUZANNE, PRESIDENT, PRIDE MOTOR GROUP 143

INTRODUCTION

I made the decision to write this book at the height of the COVID-19 pandemic. My life had changed so much in the preceding six years, and I thought I had an interesting David vs. Goliath story of determination, commitment, and hard work against seemingly insurmountable odds. Something I thought we needed during that difficult time. My childhood isn't something I like to revisit, but it wasn't until I began writing that I started to notice that the seeds of my success were planted in those early days. Like Dorothy in *The Wizard of Oz*, I had the power all along to change my life. I just didn't know it until I had the opportunity to bloom.

The stories in this book reflect the author's recollection of events. Names, locations, and identifying characteristics have been changed to protect the privacy of those depicted.

OCTOBER 19, 2014

MY DAUGHTER, ALEXANDRA, WAS A BALL OF NERVES. I couldn't blame her. We were in Burlington, Vermont, driving to the last practice before her figure skating competition, and she hadn't performed well all week. She was grumpy and irritable. Which I knew was why she had been quiet with her father when he had called her at the hotel to wish her luck and tell her he loved her.

"I gotta go," she had said.

It was strange not to hear her say she loved him back. She always did that.

When I got on the phone with Michael, who was back home in Middleton, Massachusetts, I made light of Ally's distance.

"Don't take it personally," I said. Ally was fourteen and tended to get like that before competing. It was hard for him to understand. Michael had grown up an only child and had limited experience with teenage girls.

Luckily, practice went well, and Ally's spirits were better by the time we got back into the car to return to the hotel.

As we drove, my phone rang. The screen showed the name of my son's girlfriend. I picked up.

Maggie was hysterical.

"There's a Ferrari up in flames!" she said, her voice strained. "I think it's your husband. I think Michael was killed in the accident."

"No, that can't be," I said calmly.

Maggie explained that her cousin worked at the local police department and told her about a crash that had taken place on Sycamore Street, which was a block from where we lived. A red Ferrari had hit a tree. Michael drove a red Ferrari.

I glanced at Ally, who was sitting next to me and listening to the conversation being blasted via Bluetooth in the car. I could tell she was getting nervous. "I just talked to him maybe an hour or two ago," I told Maggie. There were two other red Ferraris in Middleton; one was driven by the man who had built our home and the other by an insurance agent.

"Plus, Michael's not home." He had told me he was going out to dinner with a friend. I told Maggie not to worry, and we ended the call.

But I got a sick feeling in the pit of my stomach. And my intuition is rarely wrong.

When we arrived at our hotel, I told Ally to go inside so she could put on her makeup and dress and get ready for the competition. I said I needed to get gas and that I would be right back, but the truth was I wanted to make some more phone calls to get to the bottom of what had happened.

The rest of the evening is mostly a blur.

I remember getting out of the car to pump gas and nearly breaking my ankle tripping over the hose.

I remember it was a cold and raw night, but I was sweating, panicking, my heart racing.

I remember dialing my friend Gwen to see if she had heard anything, since Michael was supposed to be spending the evening with her husband, Samuel.

When Gwen picked up, she was very relaxed. I said to myself, *Oh, maybe I'm wrong. Maybe everything really is all right.*

Gwen had just gotten off the phone with Samuel. My dog, Winston, had taken off into the woods, and Samuel and Michael had looked for him for nearly an hour. They finally found him and fed him, and they were leaving to have dinner at a local restaurant. I told Gwen what Maggie had told me.

"No, it's not them," Gwen said plainly.

Still, I was panic-stricken. I begged Gwen to call around or drive down to Sycamore Street since she lived in the next town over. She said she would.

I finished up at the gas station and drove back to the hotel. As I parked and was getting ready to leave my car, Gwen called back.

"It's them," she said.

* * *

I don't remember how long I sat there on the sidewalk. Ten minutes? Twenty? Only that I screamed when Gwen said the words—a deep, woeful *Noooooooo!*—before I collapsed in front of the hotel. My mind played back the last conversation with Michael. What had been the last thing I said to him? I couldn't remember if I had told him I loved him after Ally didn't.

Ally.

She hadn't told him she loved him. Oh, no.

How many times have we not acted like our best self with

someone we love? How often are we short and rude and pissed off, thinking we always have another chance to make it right? This might affect Ally for the rest of her life.

I worried that she would never forgive herself.

I don't remember how I finished the call with Gwen.

And I didn't realize it would be the last time I ever spoke to her.

* * *

I called my good friend Evelyn, who was inside the hotel. Her daughter was also competing that evening. She came outside, and I told her what had happened.

Then I had to do one of the most difficult things I've ever had to do in my life: I had to call my nineteen-year-old son, Mikey, to tell him that his father was gone. Mikey was playing hockey up in British Columbia, staying with a family who had sons playing on his team. He answered the phone after only a couple of rings. When I told him, the line went quiet.

"Mikey?" I asked.

No sound.

After a few moments, I heard some movement on the other end, and the mother of Mikey's friend picked up the line.

"He passed out," she said.

Meanwhile, my daughter was about to go on the ice, and I had to deliver this devastating news. Again.

"I'm going to need help," I said to Evelyn. "Can you come with me?"

When we got to my hotel room, my daughter had her competition dress on and was putting on her makeup. I summoned my strength, trying to figure out how to say the words, but as soon as I walked in, the look on my face must have said it all. Ally took one look at me and fell to the floor. She knew.

I ran to her, trying to console her, but I could only do so much because I was still in shock, trying to get my wits about me. Nothing felt real. Luckily, my friends—the other skating moms and coaches—were there. They came into my room, and everyone hugged us as we sat and cried.

I let it all out. For hours. Balled up in a fetal position. *This couldn't be happening.*

But it *was* happening.

I let myself grieve for a little while longer, but I vowed right then and there that this would be the first and last night that I felt sorry for Suzanne Iovanna. I had to start making some decisions. I was responsible for two children and needed to figure things out. How was I going to pay the bills? How could I make sure my kids would be okay? And what about Pride Motor Group, my husband's car dealerships? The business that his parents had started decades earlier?

"What do you want to do?" I asked my kids at some point over the next few days. "Should we sell the business?"

My son was adamant. "Mom, I know it's going to be a huge undertaking, and I know I haven't gone to college yet, but my dream was always to take over the business."

How proud I was of Mikey in that moment! And scared to death. And I knew, deep in my heart, that was what Michael would have wanted too: for his son to take the reins. But Mikey was still a child. And I knew nothing about cars. Or business, for that matter. My work, long ago, had been in dental hygiene.

Still, I couldn't say no.

"All right," I said, never realizing, at that moment, that I would be put to the test and be up against insurmountable odds that would force me to challenge myself and reinvent myself. My life was about to change again, and as I figured out who I was and where I was going, I would have to look back at where I came from and remember who I used to be.

PART I

BEFORE

Chapter 1

SUZANNE, GIRL

I WAS BORN ON FEBRUARY 26, 1966, IN HALE HOSPITAL in Haverhill, Massachusetts, the oldest of the three children of John and Carolyn Mara. I was a pretty big baby—eight pounds, one ounce—which I always found pretty surprising, since I was very thin as a child.

As far back as I can remember, I was a responsible kid. I had to be. I often had to take care of my younger brother, Stephen, who was intellectually and developmentally disabled and two years younger than me.

Throughout my childhood, and especially in those early years, Stephen and I were very close. There weren't a lot of kids in my neighborhood who were his age, and because he had special needs, no one wanted to bother with him. He had only one friend named Jimmy whose brother had special needs as well, but since our family only had one car, which my dad drove to work, and Jimmy's family didn't have a car, Stephen could never have playdates. He was stuck with me.

In the 1970s, our neighborhood in Sycamore, Massachusetts, was all boys. There were no other little girls my age to play with, so I basically became a tomboy because I wanted to fit in. I did whatever the boys wanted to do because I knew they would not want to play with dolls. I spent my days building forts and playing sports—to this day, I love sports, and that's probably why. We were always playing dodgeball, kickball, baseball, whatever it was. I was coming home filthy and loving it.

One day, I think I was in fifth or sixth grade, one of the boys said, "Let's smoke a cigarette."

"Come on. We're going to the fields," another said.

At the end of my street was a massive cornfield. We played in there for hours until the streetlights came on and it was time to go home.

I was excited. I felt like I was a trusted member of the boys' club. We buried ourselves among the tall stalks and got into a circle. One of the boys lit the cigarette and passed it to the next and then the next. By the time it got to me, I took it awkwardly between my fingers, put the end to my lips, inhaled, and handed it to my younger brother, Stephen, whom I had dragged with me.

The two of us started coughing immediately.

In between hacks, though, I thought, *Wow, this feels kind of good.* I was such a straight-and-narrow kid, the oldest of three, and never deviated from what I was supposed to do. Finally, I was doing something that would not only make my parents mad but was unhealthy for me! Woo hoo! And I wasn't going to get caught! I thought, *Maybe I like this.*

The next day, we decided to try smoking again. I was ready. I didn't drag my brother along this time because I was afraid he would tell on me. Plus, I had a crush on one of the boys, Steve—tall, thin, dark-haired, really good-looking. Anytime we got together and played, I got gaga googly-eyed, and I didn't want my brother hanging around.

We hurried into the cornfield, and as soon as I put the cigarette near my mouth, I began to cough.

I couldn't do it.

I thought, *This is disgusting. I will never, ever again smoke a cigarette.* And I never did.

I often think about that euphoric feeling I had smoking that first time. Was it just the idea of being naughty that had me hooked? The idea that dependable Suzanne wasn't all that dependable? It felt good to throw caution to the wind instead of keeping anxiety bottled up inside, which was what I usually did.

Anything not to incur the wrath of my dad.

* * *

My father had bipolar disorder, which meant that when my father entered my childhood home, my mother and I didn't know which John Mara we were going to see. Some days, he came home nice as pie. Other times, well, he wasn't so nice. He wasn't physically abusive, but I suffered from emotional abuse, although I didn't know it at the time. Back then, there wasn't much discussion about mental illness, and even if you suspected you or someone you loved was dealing with it, no one admitted it.

We might be sitting down as a family at the dinner table, and he would start ranting. "Oh, this dinner is horrible. This is not what I wanted to eat. I've had a bad day." He might throw things and damage walls. He might get my mom so upset that she would cry, which made him even more furious. And when one of his moods was over, he would go back to acting normal, which made us scratch our heads.

My whole childhood I fantasized about having a different

kind of family and a different kind of life. I wanted to be like my best friend who grew up in an Italian family that always had meals together, laughed, and shared and supported one another. Don't get me wrong; when my dad was himself, he and my mom were always holding hands and doing things together. He could be calm and kind. But those times were few and far between.

My father did go to a therapist, but he lied and said what the therapist wanted to hear, which infuriated my mother. That's why he never really got better. His medications didn't work because the therapist never understood the problem, so he never adjusted or tweaked them to meet my father's needs. My father never helped himself because that was how he wanted to be.

Miserable.

Which made me miserable.

Especially at mealtimes, when we gathered as a family. I didn't want to eat. I wanted to crawl under the table. My stomach was in knots. My palms were sweaty, and my heart raced. A bomb could drop at any moment, and I had to be prepared. Constant vigilance. Although my sister might tell you that I was my father's favorite, that's little consolation when you're scared shitless all the time. Plus, it's not like my father ever took time to notice or support me and say, "Oh, Suzanne, great job," or "Hey, Suzanne, how can I help you?" "Favorite" meant that he yelled at me the least. And my mom was so focused on my brother, who had special needs, that I kind of grew up making my own way. I learned to live with the anxiety caused by my father's unpredictable moods. Channel it. Make it my own. Focus on what I could change. I think oldest children tend to be independent by nature, but for me, taking control of what I could—rearranging my room, getting jobs, and buying my own clothes—was a path to independence and a lifeline.

* * *

School wasn't much of a haven either. For some reason, my elementary school teachers called me out for being painfully shy, but actually, I was afraid of being made fun of. It's bad enough when you're frozen in fear most of the time, but when it's not acknowledged or understood, and when it's brought to others' attention, it just makes things worse.

In fourth grade, I sat behind this beautiful girl with a beautiful voice. Val was not only gorgeous in every way but also super smart. I knew I was smart, too, but I always lived with the anxiety that I wasn't smart *enough*. Or pretty *enough*. Or good *enough*. And that affected every facet of my life. My teacher would say to me, "Oh, Suzanne, too bad you don't have hair like her," or "Suzanne, it's too bad you're not as smart as her." Can you imagine? We're more on top of that kind of thing today, but back then, teachers had free rein. Their word was gospel. Especially to the elementary school children who were sitting in front of them. Most teachers, I'm sure, are well meaning, but idle comments like that can stick with children for a really long time. They certainly did with me. I felt like a failure and that I'd never make it in life.

I never got into trouble or did anything wrong. To this day, I have never even stolen a paperclip. (Meanwhile, my sister was smoking in her room and throwing the butts out the window.) Having a brother like I did and knowing how overwhelmed my mom was, I didn't think she needed another child to be rebellious or trouble. I was a good girl. I was more like her. So why, I wondered back then, were people picking on me?

My only respite in those days, other than playing outside with the boys, was going to my grandmother's house. Every week, we went for Sunday dinner, and I got really excited. My mom cooked for us every night, and she always made a dessert, like pudding, but we never had a lot of treats in the house. No soda, other than ginger ale, and we really didn't have candy unless there was a birthday or special occasion. But my grandmother had all that stuff!

My uncle had six kids, so we had tons of cousins around. I couldn't wait to get through the meal because afterward, my cousins, my aunts, and I washed all the dishes. I know that might not sound like a blast, but we formed an assembly line and wiped all the dishes down and told fun stories about what happened that week—with lots of laughing. It was like one big, happy family—something I didn't have the rest of the week with my dad, especially if it was a bad week. This was my escape. When we finished, I would think, *Okay, now Grandma is going to go for the Jax root beer!* That was my favorite. Then my grandmother always got those orange candies that looked like peanuts. I couldn't wait.

My grandmother's house was pretty large, and after dinner, the men sat on the couches and watched whatever game was on, football or hockey, and we girls sat at the dining room table—my aunts, my mom, and my grandmother sat at one end talking, and my cousins and I sat down the other end. I was in my glory. I know it sounds corny, but for me it was one of the happiest times of my life. I felt like I belonged. Like I was finally accepted for who I was. There was no judgment. I didn't have to pretend I was somebody else, and nobody made fun of how I dressed, what I ate, or what I said.

In one of the upstairs bedrooms, my grandmother had a den area with another TV, so my cousins and I, all twenty of us, piled in. It wasn't a large room, but we just sat on top of one another. Just us girls. They treated me like a queen. I felt so loved.

But that feeling never lasted long.

The ride home, particularly if my father didn't like something one of my uncles or aunts said, could be hell. I would cower in the backseat, hoping my father wouldn't get mad and direct his anger at me. This was the routine for years.

Eventually, we stopped going to my grandmother's house altogether. My dad got really nasty toward my aunts and uncles, and it was just too uncomfortable for my mom.

We also got together with my dad's family and had great times, but after they all passed on, he didn't want to see my mom's family anymore. I don't know.

Maybe it was too painful for him.

At Christmastime, we had no family around, but we had so many gifts from both sides of the family under the tree that my mom would let us open one a night before Christmas so that we could enjoy our relatives' gifts before Santa came. I guess it was the best she could do under the circumstances. Kind of like a substitute. But it just wasn't the same as going to Grandma's.

* * *

My father got on my brother, Stephen, a lot, but thank god my brother didn't know any better, so it didn't bother him. It bothered me. I'm sure my dad was disappointed he didn't have a typical son, and he lashed out at Stephen for it. Sometimes I think if Stephen had been typical, it would have been worse for him growing up.

I'd like to think I was a good sister, although I could be a bit bossy. Maybe it was my way of taking some control of my life since my dad always came down hard on me. Or maybe I was jealous because Stephen required so much attention. I made Stephen play house with me, and, of course, he was the dad I always bossed around. Sometimes I played cars or what he wanted, but not as often as I should have. Although I always stood up for my brother, I also have guilt because part of me was embarrassed that I did not have a "normal" brother.

Stephen and I were close, and still are, but I feel I could have done more for him. I could have researched his condition: The forceps damaged his brain during his birth. If I had done more, maybe he would be more advanced than he is.

Although he learned the road signs and can drive, he still cannot read and do many of the things we take for granted, but he knows certain things well. Like sports. He knows a lot of facts about teams and players. And he can be funny with people. He will find out something that a person knows—like about business or politics—and then elaborate on the topic even though he might not know what he is talking about. He doesn't get embarrassed. Just goes with the flow. I envy him for that.

My sister, Cynthia, was born when I was nine (she was a whoopsie). I was thrilled to have a sister and used to dress her up like a doll and buy her things. I was determined to give her all the things I never had while also shielding her from all my dad's negativity. I'm not sure if I was successful or if it's just the nature of genetics, but she ended up being very different from me. Confident. Outgoing. Popular. Beautiful. A hockey cheerleader. Prom queen. I was more of a wallflower. We went to the movies a few weeks ago, and she ran into a kid who was in her class in high school. He talked to her like he knew all about her, and after he left, I said, "Who was that?"

"I don't even know," Cynthia said. "Back then, I was such a snob that I only vaguely remember him." I could never imagine being surrounded by so many people that I didn't even know their names!

I was happy for Cynthia but also resentful. Yes, I wanted her to have all the things that I didn't have, but it's hard to watch someone easily get those things when you had to work so hard for them. Even though that was the plan all along. Also, Cynthia missed a lot of my dad's bad behavior simply by being born nine years after me. She won the birth-order lottery. I had some resentment there too. My dad's misery affected her, I'm sure, but not to the extent that it crushed my self-esteem. I was always so sensitive that you couldn't say anything to me without me taking it personally. And yet, in some weird silver lining, my dad's misery also taught me resilience and gave me the wherewithal to learn to fight for myself. And I would need that more than I ever knew.

Chapter 2

SUZANNE, TEEN

MY FATHER WORKED AS A MANAGER AT FRIENDLY'S ICE Cream and then Brigham's Ice Cream and made a decent living. For all the things I resent him for when I was a child, I have to give him that. He provided for us. I grew up in a four-bedroom colonial home that was very nice (my mother still lives there today). But that's not to say there was any money for extras. Or the occasional luxuries. My girlfriends took ballet classes and played instruments, but we couldn't afford that, so I felt deprived most of the time. I didn't meet a lot of girls because I couldn't participate in the finer things in life: the extracurricular activities their families could easily afford. The bright side, which I'm learning to find the older I get, is that I understood nothing in life comes easy, and if I wanted something, I had to find a way to get it myself.

When I was thirteen years old, a popular girl in my class had these Nike sneakers that I loved. I always looked up to the popular girls and wanted to be like them. I was obsessed with clothes (I still am to this day).

My mom said, "Suzanne, we can't afford them."

I talked to my best friend. "Maybe we should try to get a job."

We applied at the farmstand down her street and were both hired. In the summers, I picked vegetables and flowers to sell. In the fall, we sold pumpkins and mums, and in the winter, Christmas trees. I worked there for years.

In the summers, I had really bad hay fever, and I came home every day with watery eyes, a runny nose, and a scratchy throat. We didn't have Claritin and Zyrtec back then, and whatever I took made me tired, so I didn't want to take it.

"I'm quitting!" I declared to my mother.

"You can quit," she said, "but then you won't make money."

At that point, I had gotten used to buying things for myself. I knew what it felt like to see something in a store window and go in and buy it on a whim.

I didn't quit. I stayed with it and bought the Nikes. My first ones were white with the red swish, and I was obsessed with them. I loved the sense of independence I felt when I wore them, and I was proud of myself.

I kept working. As I got older, I worked at a salad bar, and then a clothing store till high school. I bought things for not only myself but also my sister. I was basically her second mom and gave her all the things I never had. Like a big birthday party with a Strawberry Shortcake theme. Every September, I got her a new wardrobe for the first day of school. I told her, "You'll be in style!" Like I never had been and always wanted to be.

When I was a kid, my mom had to shop for my clothing at Ann & Hope, a discount store like Walmart. Everybody else wore Levi's and cool jeans, and I was stuck with ugly skirts and lame socks. Not only was I made fun of by the teachers because I wasn't smart enough, I wasn't pretty enough, and my hair wasn't thick enough, but I was also ridiculed and bullied by my classmates for what I wore. And to top it off, I went home, and my father told me I was never going to amount to anything.

But because I didn't get a lot of pats on the back, I didn't want my sister to suffer that same lifestyle. I may not have been able to control what happened to me in elementary school, but I made sure Cynthia always had the best dress at the party.

* * *

I developed a need for perfection during this time—a consequence, probably, of my father's bipolar disorder. My childhood was chaotic. You never knew what my father would say or do. He could switch from good to bad in an instant. I'm sure some kids might have lashed out in my situation or gotten angry, but I was just scared. All the time. An anxiety that I didn't know I was having. I just knew that I had to move. Had to fix something.

This search for perfection presented itself in my room, which always had to be just so. Every few weeks, I would decide to put my bed on the other side of the room and move my furniture around. That was how I dealt with the chaos— by trying to control the things I could.

My mother would say, "What are you doing now?" "Yeah, I didn't like it there anymore" was always my answer. It was never perfect, so I was always trying to make it better. Maybe I was trying to make *me* better. To this day, I don't go to bed at night until my house is "perfect"—my daughter's dolls coordinated, my son's hockey pucks lined up in a row.

My son's friends used to go into my kitchen cabinets and rearrange all my food because my son showed them how I had to have everything just so. I would eventually change everything back to the way it made sense. At least for me.

The need for order still consumes me today.

* * *

I knew from the eighth grade that I wanted to be a dental hygienist. How weird does that sound? I have no idea why, but I always wanted to clean people's teeth. In high school, my mother suggested I work in a dental practice so that I could be sure that was what I wanted to do. I didn't listen to her, so I continued working at a clothing store, which turned out to be a mistake. (You should always listen to your mom.)

There were only a few dental hygienist schools at the time. The so-called best one was Forsyth, which was connected to Northeastern University in Boston. I didn't get into that school. I got into another one, Middlesex, a few towns over in Bedford, Massachusetts, and one in Portland, Maine, called Westbrook College, which was where I ended up going.

Westbrook was an all-girls private college. They had a few boys, but they were international students. The school offered two-year, three-year, and four-year programs. During a weekend when prospective students could visit to see if they liked the college, I met my roommate, Ellen, on the bus ride there. She was very outgoing, a cheerleader, and lived in the next town over from me. She was everything I wanted to be, and we just hit it off. She had decided to attend Westbrook's three-year program, but my parents said they could only afford two years of college, so that was what I ended up doing.

It was a rigorous schedule. I attended classes, did clinics, and worked on patients from 8:00 a.m. to 9:00 p.m. every weekday, essentially trying to complete four years of school in two.

The first semester, I almost failed. In my very first class, Dental Anatomy, I was the only one who failed one test because everyone else had worked in a dental office. They knew every tooth in the mouth. They knew what an X-ray was. I didn't know anything. That first semester, my advisor sat down with me and said, "Suzanne, if you don't improve your grades, you're not going to stay in this program."

Of course, that sent my dad through the roof.

It wasn't like I was partying. It wasn't a party school. The biggest thing on the weekends was to walk down to the Chinese restaurant, get some lo mein, and then go home and study some more.

The problem was that I had always been a terrible test taker. On an average school day, I was already an incredibly nervous person, but on days I had exams, I got panic attacks. I'd sweat, and my heart would feel like it was pounding out of my chest. My whole body would shake. I could have known the material inside out and upside down, but my mind would go blank. Every time. And because I knew I was going to freeze up, all day long leading up to the test, I couldn't relax.

But I managed to get it together and pass my classes.

When it came time to study for my National Board Dental Hygiene Examination, one of the many steps and require-ments for licensure and becoming a dental hygienist, my nerves were off the charts. My mom—who'd never given me a drug in my life—had some pills for my brother in the medicine cabinet. Sometimes he was all over the place before bed and needed them to slow down and unwind.

"You should take one of these," my mom told me.

Not knowing what else to do, I took them. And they made things even worse.

When I arrived at the test site and began the exam, not only did my mind go blank, but I had a hard time settling down. The pills had the opposite effect on me that they had on my brother. I freaked out worse than ever. After I finished the test, I called my mother and cried hysterically.

The day I graduated from college, I went home and got the test results back. I had failed.

By one point.

Instantly, my dad laid into me.

"I can't believe this. We spent all this money we don't even have," he ranted.

I felt terrible. I knew I could've passed the test if I'd just relaxed. I had managed to secure a highfalutin job at a large, world-renowned dental practice and teaching facility beginning the following fall, but now I wasn't going to be able to keep it because I had failed my boards.

Every day that summer, I woke up early in the morning and, after going to church, headed straight to the library to study before work at the clothing store. By the end of the summer, I retook my boards and got a ninety.

Failure hadn't devastated me. It had lit a fire under me.

I was beginning to understand the difference.

Chapter 3

SUZANNE, WORKING GIRL

RIGHT AFTER I PASSED MY BOARDS, I STARTED MY JOB at The Perico Group, a big, world-renowned dental practice and teaching facility in Swampscott, Massachusetts. It was an honor to be working there right out of college. But with that honor came a lot of hard work. The building was three floors, and I spent most of my days running up and down stairs.

I cleaned people's teeth all day long, from 7:30 a.m. to about 6:30 p.m. Never took lunch. My diet consisted of yogurt, granola, and a banana or an apple. Five days a week. Very, very intense. Turns out, though, that kind of schedule worked for me. (I'm not a good sit-around person. Even on vacation, it takes me a day to acclimate.) The days were long, but I loved it. I loved having patients. I loved improving their health. I loved getting to know them. Our clientele included a lot of famous people, too, like Senator Ted Kennedy.

After being there for a few years, one of the hygienists, who was also a surgical assistant, became pregnant and told the dentist she was working with that I would be the perfect candidate to replace her, which ruffled a few feathers because

I was one of the younger hygienists and hadn't been there very long.

I said to her, "Well, it's great that you have the confidence in me, but I have never had confidence in myself, and I don't like blood."

She said, "No, I really think you can do this."

Her belief in me made me think I could do it, so I decided to give it a try.

The first time I watched a surgery, I said, "Yep, I'm going down," and sure enough, I fainted—which is kind of embarrassing when you're trying to impress your bosses. Still, they believed in me and said I should try again, so I went in to assist for another surgery—and down I went again!

"I'm telling you guys," I said. "Call my mom. Once I jammed both my fingers in a chair, and they were bleeding, and I needed stitches. I fainted. She fainted. I'm not sure this is going to work."

When I was cleaning someone's mouth, sure, there was a little blood, but it wasn't gushing—and you weren't cutting all their gums and tissues and exposing them.

"No, you can do it!" they said.

Luckily, the third time was the charm. I don't know what happened. Something just clicked. I tried focusing on the procedure rather than the patient—on what the doctors were doing rather than the person they were doing it on. I was so fascinated by what the human bone looked like and what disease looked like. As a hygienist, I knew that bacteria grew when you didn't floss, and I knew bad things happened when you didn't get your teeth cleaned properly. I could take an X-ray and tell the doctor, "Hey, they have a five-millimeter pocket, so I think they're going to need surgery." But I'd never seen the tissue brought down to exposed bone. I was fascinated at the amount of bone loss caused by poor oral hygiene and at what was required to repair it.

Then the woman I had covered for decided she wasn't coming back after her maternity leave, and they asked me to be the permanent assistant for this doctor. It was a lot to think about. All these years, I had wanted to be a hygienist. I had put in so much time and effort. I had done well on the boards, and everything was finally starting to click. I had only been at the practice for about three years. But I was so intrigued by everything I was learning and really enjoyed this new experience, so I said, "All right, I'll give it a go."

And I never really looked back.

* * *

Not long after I became a surgery assistant at the dental practice, the doctor I assisted told me, "Well, now you're in the big seat. You have to start teaching as well."

At the time, I could barely go into a room and start talking to someone who was right next to me. Nothing had changed since childhood. I felt like I wasn't good enough. I didn't want to be judged. Extremely shy was an understatement. "Oh, I don't know," I said.

"Suzanne, you have to start doing things that aren't in your comfort zone."

I thought I already was! But if the girl who fainted at the first sight of blood could stand on two feet during a complex dental surgery, maybe she could stand in front of a crowded room and speak too.

At that time, we conducted a lot of big, breakthrough surgeries right there in our office—procedures that were usually done in a hospital setting. Because my facility was large, we could accommodate several assistants. One assistant worked next to the doctor, in the mouth, peeling the gums away and getting the mouth ready for the implant. A hygienist or surgical assistant stood behind the doctor and handed him instruments or whatever he needed. Sometimes, we also hired an anesthesiologist to come into the practice, but if we didn't, a third assistant communicated with the patient ("Are you all right? Is there anything you need?"), took down vitals during the procedure, and took care of pre- and post-op.

I began attending seminars in Boston to teach other doctors how to perform various procedures. For example, I went around to the doctor-participants and said, "This is what your assistant should be doing. This is how your assistant should dress."

I was facing my fears and not only learning to be comfortable as a teacher, as someone others could learn from, but enjoying it as well.

Surprisingly, I didn't miss being a hygienist at all.

Chapter 4

SUZANNE, GIRLFRIEND

I WASN'T A BIG DATER IN COLLEGE. I HAD ONE BOY-friend, Jay, who I met through a friend. He came from a rich town, and his dad was a big-time lawyer. He went to a private school in Maine and had his own apartment. One of my girlfriends knew him and introduced us, and he asked me out. He had just broken up with his girlfriend, which should have been a red flag, but he was tall, blond, and handsome, and the other girls at my all-girl college were so jealous of me, so I couldn't say no. But I was so nervous! I only dated one boy in high school, and that barely counted. He was my neighbor. I went to his prom, and he came to mine. He liked me, but I only thought of him as a friend.

Jay was really cute. When he visited me at my dorm, the RA had to buzz him in, and she would ask, "Who are you here to see?"

All the girls would run downstairs, saying things like, "Oh, Suzanne's so lucky!"

They thought I was lucky, so I must have been, right?

I was really falling for him.

One day my parents came up for the day. They were supposed to meet Jay, but he had an "emergency" at the last minute and had to go home. He later came to me with a big bouquet of flowers to apologize, and we got together a few more times, but he ended up getting back together with his ex-girlfriend (who I think was the "emergency").

I was pretty devastated. I thought I was going to marry that guy.

I continued to study almost full time. I squeezed four years of college into two. It wasn't until I started working full time that my weekends became footloose and fancy free. A girlfriend I met in college and I became best friends, working together from 7:30 a.m. to 6:30 p.m. every day, and we were ready to let loose on the weekends and bar hop. It was like I was living my college days even though I was out of college and had a full-time job.

I never really drank too much, but I don't know how we got through that period alive. We looked like "butanas," as my father would say, with our hair a mile high and our short skirts and high heels. Everyone dressed that way back then. Although I was still shy, once I was on the dance floor, my shyness left me. I credit my girlfriend with helping to bring me out of my shell.

I also credit a group of guys we met from Quincy, Massachusetts (we lived on the north shore of Boston). They reminded me of the boys I hung out with growing up. Just fun. I ended up dating one of them (he had just broken up with his girlfriend too—another red flag!), but that fizzled.

After that, I went out with a few guys, but nothing serious. My experience with dating was limited, but I'd always been interested in sports and comfortable with boys, and my guy-friend relationships as an adult gave me confidence.

Confidence to ask out a cute guy I met at a car dealership.

* * *

In 1988, I had been driving a 1970 Chevy Nova for four years. It was a piece of junk, but it was all my parents could afford to get me. Any time it rained or you went through massive puddles, you had to get out and spray WD-40 on the wires. Which I did many times at two in the morning with my girlfriends—in our short skirts and high heels, coming home from a club.

Anyway, this car finally broke down, and since I was making money now at the dental practice, my dad said, "Okay, you can afford a new car. I'll take you to a dealer I know." At the time, he was working at Friendly's, and one of his regulars was a big Nissan dealer principal.

Needless to say, my first car was a Nissan. A Sentra.

I had that car for maybe a year, and I was going to work one day and took a different route to avoid the traffic because I wanted to get there earlier. I had a stop sign, but I didn't see it and went through it, and another car hit me. My car was totaled.

Luckily, nobody was hurt, but I had to tell my parents. And I needed a new car. A lot of my friends had Mercury Cougars, and I had decided that if anything happened to my car, that was what I wanted to get. My dad said, "I don't know if you'll be able to afford this. And I don't know if this is a good car." I didn't care. I was getting a Mercury Cougar. (What's funny is that, at the time, my roommate had a Hyundai, which is one of the dealerships I have now, but back then a Hyundai was the last car I wanted.)

There was a Lincoln Mercury dealership nearby, and I

went late one night with my girlfriend. We were walking the lot, and I found the car I wanted: a brand-new 1988 Mercury Cougar. It was black with a red interior. We went back the next day and worked with a man named Michael, who I thought was the salesperson but turned out to be the vice president. And also my future husband.

When I went to sign all the paperwork, Michael asked me, "What are you doing for the Super Bowl? I'm having a Super Bowl party if you want to come."

"No, I don't think so."

I wasn't sure if I liked him. I was twenty-two years old and not looking for anything serious, so I basically bought the car and left. But I had to go back to the dealership for paperwork another day and thought, *You know what? I think I'm going to go out with him.*

When I saw Michael, I said, "Hey, do you wanna go out to dinner or something like that?"

"Are you asking me out?" he asked.

"Well, you asked me to your Super Bowl party, but I couldn't make it, so yeah, I guess I am." (That was always the big joke later on. "Mom, you asked Dad out!" my kids would say. Michael couldn't wait to tell people, "You should meet my wife. She asked me out first.")

He bought me a rose, and took me to dinner, and we went somewhere after. But late in the evening, a guy I knew came up and started talking to me, and Michael got jealous. Angry, even. I thought, *I just met you. Am I just supposed to ignore a friend of mine?*

I thought he was being a jerk, and I didn't think I'd ever go out with him again. I couldn't wait to get home and tell my roommate that I wasn't going to see him again. She even thought Michael was snobby.

But the next day at work, I got a dozen roses.

I thought, *Well, maybe I'll give him another shot.*

And then another month in, he bought me a tennis bracelet.

I know it sounds shallow that expensive gifts were causing me to have a change of heart. But it wasn't the roses or the bracelet that turned me on. It was knowing that someone wanted to buy me something. That I was worthy of nice things. I felt validated. I'd never had that before.

As we dated over the next few weeks, Michael continued to surprise me with gifts. One day he said, "Oh, I'm just going to take your car for a day. I think it has a leak," and then put a half roof in because he knew I always wanted one and couldn't afford it.

I was so flattered, and at the time I didn't even know that he owned the car dealership. I just thought he was a really nice guy who had a big heart and wanted to help people. He bought me things, wined and dined me. I felt like a princess. I'd never had a boyfriend like that. I'd hardly had any boyfriends at all! In a lot of ways, Michael was really my first serious relationship.

So you can imagine my surprise when, after only dating for eight weeks, Michael proposed.

Even more surprising? I said yes.

* * *

When your only son comes home and says, "Hey, I got engaged," and you find out he proposed to a girl after only two months of dating, you pretty much assume she's a gold digger. Or maybe pregnant.

That was Michael's parents' first impression of me.

I didn't blame them. They didn't know anything about me.

And since they both came from a hardscrabble background and had worked very hard to get where they were, they both basically said, "Um, no, you're not marrying her." My parents were the same. (Not because they thought Michael was a gold digger. We didn't have much money.)

The first few times I met Michael's parents were rough—not his dad so much, but his mother. She was very protective of him and seemed to go out of her way to be difficult (it's strange to look back and think about her in this way, since she eventually became one of my best friends). She kept picking on me, saying things like, "Oh, you're so quiet."

I remember going to get boneless spare ribs, pork fried rice, and crab rangoon from a place called Fantasy Island down the street from where they lived on a Friday night. They always had Chinese food on Fridays. I was sitting in her kitchen before she got home, just staring at the detailing on the old brown, intricate cabinets because I was so nervous about the comments she might make. It was like eating dinner at home all over again. My hands were sweating. I was too nervous to eat—a childhood trait that continues to plague me. Although Michael's mother was thin, too, she always made comments about how much I ate or didn't eat ("Oh, you're not eating?") or the number of hours I worked ("You work all those hours? They should be giving you a lunch. That's against the law. We'd never do that at my dealership"). Everything I talked about—politics, the weather—was wrong.

I thought, *What am I doing? I left my house to get away from this kind of stuff!*

It went on like that for almost a year.

I don't blame my mother-in-law for being that way. She wanted her son to marry a boisterous, loud person like he was. The life of the party. That just wasn't me. At the time, I thought that was a problem. That something was probably wrong with me. She eventually got to know me and my parents, and we all became very good friends, but she died when I was still shy and insecure. She doesn't know the person I became.

Back then, Michael's parents said they would give our marriage their blessing if we stayed engaged for two years. My parents told us the same.

We agreed.

And that was when the trouble started.

Michael and I began to fight. All the time. All throughout that first year. He suggested that we break up. Maybe he knew something I didn't, but at the time I didn't think he was serious. I still believed that we were engaged and wore my ring. I was raised to believe that you stuck with things, and with people, even if there were hardships. My mom taught me that. Whether it was my brother or my dad or a profession.

One day, at a big fair in a town called Topsfield, my sister saw Michael with his old girlfriend. He had begun dating her while we were, technically, still together. I thought the world was going to end. I remember going to my mother-in-law and telling her that he was cheating on me. (Michael was mad at my sister for a long time for telling me.)

Looking back, it's so strange that I confided so much in my mother-in-law. I had other friends to talk to and hang out with when Michael and I had our troubles, but my mother-in-law and Michael's aunt had become like a second family to me. I always felt much older on the inside since I'd had to help my mom care for my brother when I was a kid and I had practically raised my sister. Maybe that was why I related to my mother-in-law and her sisters. I spent a lot of time with them shopping at Marshall's and then going out for Chinese or Japanese food.

They advised me on what to do.

"You have to pretend that you don't care," his aunt said.

"You're gonna have to give him space," my mother-in-law told me. "He has never fallen hard for anyone like you. I know he loves you, and I love you like a daughter."

Their feelings for me probably got in the way of their objectivity. And mine too.

But for better or for worse, they talked me through it. For the entire two years of the engagement, I didn't date anyone, but Michael continued to stray. At one point, we had broken up, and once more, he went back to his ex-girlfriend. I thought, *Here we go again!* Then Michael and I got back together, and my insecurities kicked into high gear. Every time we got into a fight, I asked him, "Are you leaving me for her?"

It was a rocky engagement to say the least, but despite it all, two years later, as planned, we got married. I had hoped that marriage would solve all my trust issues. That I would finally be happy. But I would soon learn that secrets don't just go away. They fester. Especially if you don't go looking for them.

Chapter 5

SUZANNE, WIFE AND MOTHER

MICHAEL AND I GOT MARRIED ON MAY 27, 1990, AND not surprisingly, our first year of marriage was rough. A lot of that had to do with one thing: I didn't realize I had married a person who was addicted to cocaine.

To this day, I'm not sure how I didn't suspect it. I guess Michael hid it well. The guys I used to hang out with from Quincy smoked weed and did cocaine, but that was so clear to me. Their behavior was obvious. They could be erratic. Have sudden spikes in energy. Slur their words.

Michael was different. He seemed fine. I had no idea he was doing cocaine. (To make matters worse, drugs ran rampant through the car dealership. My in-laws were clueless.) The only reason I found out about Michael was we were living in a townhouse at the time, and a woman contacted me to try to collect our condo fee. "I can't get in touch with your husband," she told me. "You haven't paid your condo fee in, like, six months."

"What are you talking about?" I asked.

Michael wanted us to keep our money separate. When we got married, he said, "Listen, you're a hygienist. You have your own money. You can buy whatever you want. That's your money. I'll pay the bills and do the savings." I never knew, till the day my husband died twenty-four years later, what our finances were like. Never saw a bill. Never paid the mortgage. Never even knew what the payments were—and we lived in three or four homes over the course of our marriage. I let Michael take care of everything (a mistake that I am making sure my daughter will never make).

Here I was, a new wife, with a husband who was not only addicted to cocaine, but now he was never home. He worked all day and stayed out until two o'clock in the morning. When I asked him where he was, he would give me a song and dance about working late at the dealership, and then the next day I would get roses or other flowers from the florist. Just like when we were dating. Presents. And more presents. This happened every time he was in the doghouse.

When I found out that Michael hadn't paid the condo fee, I called my mother-in-law, and she was as shocked as I was. "What do you mean he hasn't paid the fee?" She paid it for me because I didn't have a checkbook, and then she came over and we did a little investigating. We went into Michael's closet and found not only his checkbook and hollowed-out pens (to snort coke), but also rolled-up dollars and other drug paraphernalia.

One night when he went out, I followed him. He was with three of his friends, and at first I just thought they were all drunk, but then I saw them getting high too. I caught them in the act.

My in-laws and I decided to have an intervention.

We reached out to Michael's managers at the dealership and sat down with them and Michael. My in-laws said to him, "If you don't go to rehab, you're going to be cut out of everything. The will. The dealership. Everything."

"Everyone does cocaine," Michael said with a sneer. "I'm not addicted."

But he agreed to go to rehab for six months. After that, to my knowledge, he never touched cocaine again. I never told anybody, not even my parents. If anyone asked where Michael was during that time, I'd lie. I was so embarrassed. To this day, my mother thinks Michael had an alcohol problem, and I only recently told my sister. I thought that part of our life was over. I had no idea that Michael's addiction would find other outlets. Like alcohol. And Ambien.

* * *

When I got pregnant in 1993, even though it was three years after Michael had gotten out of rehab, my mother-in-law was upset with us because she thought it was too soon. But I was elated.

Soon after I became pregnant with Mikey, my bosses at the dental practice approached me about traveling to Germany to teach dental assistants about some of the new advances in surgery. The doctors in our practice had been traveling to Europe to train dentists there, while others came to our teaching facility in the States. Because I was a nervous traveler—I didn't like going anywhere alone—my husband said he would come with me.

This alleviated some of my anxiety but produced some anxiety as well. Michael hadn't been out of rehab for very long, and I wasn't sure he was up for the trip. But I was also excited. I had never been on a plane before and felt like I was finally expanding my horizons.

Although my boss and his wife sat in first class, I was in economy. Back then, airlines had smoking rows and non-smoking rows, and Michael and I were in the last row of the non-smoking section, so it wasn't a surprise that the guys sitting right behind us were smoking.

"Can you put out your cigarettes, please?" Michael said loudly. "My wife's pregnant."

Of course, the guys behind us pretended they didn't speak English, and they smoked the entire way to Germany. I remember thinking, *I'm overtired. I'm stuck with smoke. My child is gonna come out, and my husband is going to punch someone.*

As soon as we got to Germany, my boss said, "Let's go right to the office." Then it was surgery, teach, surgery, teach. And since Europeans ate dinner late, I didn't get to bed until midnight. That first night, I thought I might pass out in my dinner.

Michael stayed home for the next trip, but that didn't relieve my anxiety. I wasn't eating or sleeping, and with that rigorous schedule, I had trouble focusing and was miserable. All I could think was, *Just let me sleep for an hour.* But every night, just as I was falling asleep, the new day was beginning with the company sending someone to pick me up bright and early.

After Mikey was born, I continued to travel. I went back to Germany three or four times over the next couple of years and then started going to Italy. Sometimes Michael came. Sometimes he didn't. But as a new mom, my anxiety became even worse. My mind raced. What if something happened to Mikey while I was gone? I would call my mother, and she would tell me to relax. "He doesn't even know you're gone," she said. That made me feel worse.

I was so torn. I was assisting cutting-edge surgeries at my job and feeling like I was a part of something important while also wanting to be with my child. I tried keeping my hours down a little bit during Mikey's first year, and my mom really stepped up and helped me take care of him because my mother-in-law was working at the dealership. It helped that my son's nursery school was located diagonally across from my office, so in a pinch I could always pick Mikey up and bring him to work. But I felt like I was no good anywhere. When I was with Mikey, I worried about the office. And when I was at work, I worried about Mikey and felt guilty for not being there with him.

But when I got pregnant again, my worrying went off the charts.

* * *

Mikey was two when I got pregnant with another boy. Michael and I named him Alexander. At the time, we were renting a condo in Swampscott, and when I found out I was pregnant, we decided to buy a home. We were in the process of moving in when I was about six months pregnant and needed to have an ultrasound. For some reason, Michael couldn't go with me that day, although he went to all my appointments for Mikey, so I went by myself.

After my exam, the technician said, "I need to talk to you after this." It was kind of weird. She didn't even take me into her office. We stood in the hallway as she said, "Your baby is not going to make it."

"What are you talking about?" I said. "I heard the heartbeat. I saw him."

"I know," she said. "He has a heartbeat, and you did see him, but he has a disease where he is not growing properly."

Turns out, Michael and I carry a certain chromosome that, together, passed down a severe type of spina bifida to our baby.

"You need to go to a specialist," she said.

The specialist explained that I could go through with the pregnancy, the full forty weeks, but they didn't know if either my child or I would survive. Both of our lives would be at risk. If we both survived, there was a strong possibility that Alexander would be paralyzed or have other physical challenges. He could live a month or a year, but they said he wouldn't have a long life.

"If it was my wife," the specialist said, "I would counsel her to have an abortion."

Michael went ballistic. He couldn't believe something was wrong with our baby. He thought the doctors were lying. "No. There has to be another way."

"There is no other way," the specialist said.

I sat there, stunned. It was like words were being spoken around me, but I had no idea what they meant. And I felt whatever opinion I had about the matter wasn't valid. Along with Michael, the specialist and technician were deciding my fate. They understood the risks better than I did. In the end, I agreed with the specialist and had the procedure. What made the whole thing even worse was that they sent me to Massachusetts General, which was a teaching hospital, so they brought in students to give me an epidural, which they botched, so I was on my back for about a month after that.

Even though Michael balked at the idea of the abortion, we agreed, as a couple, to have the procedure. But he admitted to me later that he thought I did the wrong thing.

Michael and I should have gone to therapy right away. We didn't. Our relationship became strained.

I felt alone.

I remember hearing all the nurses talking about me at the hospital. "How could she do this? What a terrible mother." Their words haunted me. They still do. I thought maybe the nurses and Michael were right, that I had done the wrong thing, even though I was following my doctor's strong recommendation. He had been adamant. To this day, I harbor a lot of guilt.

We had a little funeral for Alexander after the procedure, and I got to hold him. He looked just like Mikey, which was hard. I remember sitting in the back seat of my car, feeling like my head was about to fall off. I thought, *Well, that's okay. You should feel bad because this is your punishment.* I don't know why, but throughout my life that's how I've viewed things: that I deserve the bad things that happen to me. I still struggle with that today.

I didn't want to have another baby. It was too much to go through, and I worried the same thing would happen again. I didn't want to have sex. I became so nervous. Sex had been deteriorating for us anyway—I suspected Michael had been having affairs—and this just made our love life worse.

But time has a way of making you forget. Three years after I lost my little boy, I decided I wanted another baby. I didn't want Mikey to be an only child. I saw Michael's loneliness, and he agreed. "We can't just have one child. It's not fair," he said.

I got pregnant again, and despite my fears, when my daughter, Alexandra, was born, she was perfect. She became my saving grace through those sad years following the abortion, which I never told anyone about. I told people half-truths, that Alexander's disease had ended the pregnancy. We showed people the medical reports that concluded that he probably wouldn't have survived or that I would've died. But even as I said the words, I was ashamed at what I had done.

Once I became pregnant with Alexandra, my husband said, "What about work? You can stay home if you like."

But I knew the decision had already been made, and I was fine with it. I was ready to be a stay-at-home mom.

* * *

Motherhood came naturally to me, maybe because I had spent so many years caring for my brother and sister. And also because I had learned what *not* to do. My mother is the sweetest person, but she didn't know how to be supportive of my goals and never taught me how to defend myself against what I would be up against in life, so I was determined, in many ways, to be what my mother wasn't. I took an active role in my children's education. I made sure my children knew how to be thoughtful, caring, and organized. I made sure they were well rounded by enrolling them in many sports and activities—karate, hockey, baseball, cheerleading, skating. I wanted them to find what made them happy, who they were. I wanted to allow them to enjoy and experience things in their life that I didn't.

Michael, for all his faults as a husband, was a great dad. He formed special bonds with both of his children. He and Mikey spent lots of time together through sports, and he and Ally made time for one another when they could. For instance, they both loved scary movies, so on Friday nights, or whatever night we didn't have hockey or figure skating, they would get Sour Patch Kids and Twizzlers and have scary movie marathons. They had a lot of similar traits—both were outgoing and good-natured. So often I look at Ally and see Michael.

Michael and Mikey were like brothers. Very close. It was like the brother that Michael never had. They were together all the time, and Michael even formed special bonds with Mikey's friends.

Mikey and I also had a special bond because when he was a baby and a toddler, Michael worked so much that I was the only parent around. Mikey and I liked to watch James Bond and action movies together.

I often think how sad it is that Michael will never get to see what our children have become. And will become. He would have been so proud. And despite all our problems, I would like to think he would be proud of me too.

But we did have our problems. Parenthood didn't change that. And after years of suspicion, they finally came out into the open.

* * *

Around the time we were celebrating our twentieth wedding anniversary, I learned that Michael had been having an affair with a woman named Polly, whose son had played hockey with Mikey in grammar school.

How did this happen? Like many couples, it happened over time. Often, couples drift apart, I guess. In the case of Michael and me, I'm not sure we ever drifted together. Our interests had always been so different. We didn't have a sport or a hobby that we liked to do together. I played tennis, but Michael wasn't interested. He liked motorcycles, but I wasn't interested. That was part of our problem. We didn't have anything we bonded over.

In his spare time, Michael drove Mikey to private school, picked him up, took him to hockey practice, took him and his friends to dinner, and then drove everyone home because most of the other boys' parents worked. Mikey became Michael's life.

I totally understood because my daughter had become my life. I was on the gerbil wheel with Ally—homeschooling and driving her to Boston and elsewhere for skating. While the four of us always tried to be together at the end of the day, I guess that just wasn't enough. Michael and I also tried to go out once a month, just the two of us or with friends, but *whose* friends always became an issue. Mine weren't cool enough for him. He wanted me to go out with him. But I didn't budge. And he didn't budge. And that was where we stayed.

For years, it went on this way, and it worked somehow, or so we thought. Maybe because Michael didn't need anything else for a long while. He had his parents, his wife, his kids, his friends, his business.

My mother-in-law died of lung and bone cancer in 2007. After my father-in-law had a stroke, Michael went to the nursing home every day, all day, until his father passed away in 2009. I truly believe that's the moment when I began to lose my husband. Perhaps Michael was beginning to contemplate his own mortality and feel depressed. I don't know. He never confided in me. Another problem. My husband was an only child and had now lost both of his parents.

Then my son got his driver's license, which is an exciting time for a family, but it also meant that he didn't need Michael to chauffeur him around anymore. Mikey was developing his own life. I sometimes wonder whether my husband would still be alive today if Mikey had been younger then. Mikey would have still needed his driving services, and Michael wouldn't have felt so untethered. Or maybe that would have just postponed the inevitable.

Sensing Michael's loneliness, I tried making suggestions. "Why don't you volunteer?" I said to him. "You love kids. Open a ward for women at the hospital. Something in your mother's name. Advocate for lung cancer."

He always said no. Instead, he would get up each day, go to the gym, start drinking by 2:00 p.m., and then come home.

"Do you want to take Ally to skate?" I'd ask.

"No, I have to go into work and sign checks," he'd say.

I tried and tried to get him to do things, but he never would. And with me gone all day with Ally, by 11:00 a.m., he was bored.

He had a Harley-Davidson motorcycle, and I was always petrified to go on it with him because Michael was such a risk-taker. I always thought, *God forbid something happens to me. What would happen to my kids?* Growing up in the automotive business, Michael had been driving cars since he was twelve, so while I was a nervous nelly, he liked to live on the edge. That's why I think we were attracted to one another. We were complete opposites. But while that may be exciting and wonderful at the beginning of a marriage, for us it wasn't enough to sustain one.

And it was that motorcycle that brought Michael and Polly together. Michael started riding his bike during the week and on the weekends, and he and Polly reconnected through a group of couples, including Samuel and Gwen, who didn't have Harleys but were friends with people who did. They went for rides, and my guess is Michael told Polly how miserable his marriage was, and she said the same about hers.

Suddenly, I was alone on the weekends, and on weekdays

he was coming home in the wee hours of the morning clearly drunk.

"I know something is going on," I said.

He denied it. Like I was cuckoo. Classic gaslighting.

My tried-and-true anxiety kicked in, and I began withdrawing. *What's going to happen? Am I going to have to go back to work? Will I have to get a divorce?*

Michael and I grew even more distant. We never talked—nothing more than "Oh, let's meet here for dinner and have a few drinks." He never called me during the day unless he needed something. And I pretty much stopped seeing friends socially. How could I? I had nothing to talk about. And I was embarrassed. I thought my husband was having an affair—he was never home, and I was watching football and hockey and basketball alone. As a way to get some sanity, I often took Ally to our house on the Cape.

In September 2012, I was at the Cape house with Ally, who had asked her friend to come along. After I dropped them off to eat somewhere, I finished cleaning the sheets, changing the beds, and doing other chores. I don't know what possessed me to call Michael, but I did.

And *she* answered.

"I told you to never, never answer my phone!" I heard Michael scream in the background.

Then the line disconnected. And when he called me back, he was really nasty.

Still, though, he denied having an affair. Just made up some dumb story about why a woman had answered his phone.

And it continued this way for months. Michael came home late at night, and I just slept in another room. I mean, life had to go on, right? I had to make my kids breakfast and make it through the day somehow. Michael became like a roommate. We were not together in a marital sense. We did nothing together socially. And yet he made it seem like life was wonderful. "Hey, hon!" he'd chirp when he got home. I didn't argue. I figured, *What am I gonna do?*

But it got worse. He came home more and more intoxicated. Also, when Michael's dad died, he couldn't sleep and had nightmares, so his doctor put him on a low dose of Ambien. But now he had lost weight because he was going to the gym so much, and his drinking was progressing, and he was continuing to take the same dosage of Ambien. He would stumble frantically into the room like a drug addict, demanding, "Where is my Ambien?" Then he would take one, fall asleep, and wake me up at 3:00 a.m., shouting things like, "You're a whore! You're going to wind up with nothing! I'm going to see to it that you can't divorce me!"

I would shake. I used to be that dead sleeper who, once I turned over, didn't move, but now I was shaking. Like when I was a little girl living in my father's house.

And always, the next morning, Michael would wake up and say, "Hey, Suzanne! What are you and Ally doing today?"

I would ask, "Do you remember what you said to me last night?

"No."

When I told him, he would dismiss me. "You're out of your mind. I would never say that."

One night, Ally's friends slept over. My attic was a huge playroom, so the girls slept there, and Michael became so agitated that I ran into the basement so the girls wouldn't hear all the screaming. And for the first time, as we argued, he pushed me.

"You're having an affair." "No, I'm not."

One time, I heard him talking to Polly in my bedroom on

his phone. "Don't worry. I love you. I gotta get out of here." When I confronted him, he still denied it.

I felt so alone. No one knew. The one close friend I confided in didn't believe me: "Oh, Michael's all talk, no action." I was so ashamed. I didn't even tell my sister.

But the longer it went on, the uglier it got. Michael started getting nasty to me during the day.

I would say, "You never spend time with me anymore. How come you have to go?"

"Why would I want to spend time with you?" he'd ask. "I don't even like being with you. You're boring."

"Oh, I'm boring because I don't like getting drunk every day like you? Then why are we together?"

But I knew the answer: While Michael didn't want me, he didn't want anyone else to have me.

Meanwhile, there wasn't much of me to have. I wasn't eating because my stomach was a wreck. I was paper thin. My anxiety was through the roof as I played detective, trying to find evidence of Michael's deceit. Suspicious behavior, like how he would put my seat onto his motorcycle when he went away with his motorcycle buddies for the weekend—even though I wasn't going with him.

I decided I needed to break into his phone. The next time he passed out, I tried to get the proof I needed, but I couldn't unlock it. I tried over and over, night after night, and finally one night I cracked the code. Hallelujah! And I hit the mother lode. There were so many photos of him and Polly. And then there were the texts.

I have your shirt on. I wish you were here with me.

I was right. I felt validated, yet I wanted to vomit. Then I did something that I'll always regret. I ran into my son's room and ranted.

"Your father is having an affair! I knew it!"

When Michael found out I had gone through his phone, he tackled me to the ground, shouting, "You have no right!"

But finally, the next morning, he admitted it.

"You have to leave," I said.

He went to the Cape house for two days. Then he called and said he wanted to work things out.

"We need serious therapy and counseling," I said.

I let him come back, and we started going to a therapist, but Michael's heart wasn't really in it. Truthfully, neither was mine.

Michael had come back to the family for the kids. Not for me. I knew it killed him to hurt Mikey and Ally. He loved them so much, even though sometimes he put Mikey through the wringer when it came to hockey. He could be mentally abusive, berating Mikey the whole car ride home if he didn't play well. I would turn around and see that my daughter would be riddled with anxiety during those car trips, just like I had been when I was coming home from my grandmother's house as a little girl. But, despite his faults, Michael was their dad, and they loved him.

Nine years later—about seven years after Michael was killed—I found out that Mikey knew the whole time that his father was having an affair. After hockey practice, Michael often took Mikey to an Italian restaurant that I wasn't fond of when I couldn't join them for dinner. Polly was the bartender there. She would show up "accidentally." It was an easy excuse: "Hey, I saw a friend at the restaurant!"

My son said he told Michael, "Let's get out of here," but Michael would say, "Hey, Polly, come over to our table." I felt terrible that my son had to live with that. That his father exposed him to that.

I found out later that a lot of people knew about the affair. And didn't tell me. They saw Michael and Polly out together. I'm friendly with a woman who lived in the downstairs apartment of my in-laws' house. She saw Michael in a restaurant with Polly. She went right up to him, and his response? "Oh, this is Polly." He wasn't shy about it. Hiding in plain sight.

"What are you doing?" she told me she said to him. But she didn't say a word to me then. And now the damage was done.

Michael's affair has affected every relationship I've had since—with lovers but also with friends. The one thing I value most in a relationship is trust, something that took so long for me to build after living with my father, and that was taken away from me. To this day, when I meet someone new, old insecurities pop back up. *Can I really trust this person? Will this person hurt me?* And up goes that shield. Little did I know that after Michael's death, my fears about people and their motivations would only intensify.

And with good reason.

PART II

AFTER

Chapter 6

SUZANNE, WIDOW

I WAS IN MY HOTEL ROOM IN VERMONT, REELING FROM the news of the sudden death of my husband, my mind flooded with worry. Michael and I didn't have a fairy-tale marriage by any means, but our lives were intertwined, and I had our children to think about. I had made the decision to take over Pride, Michael's trio of car dealerships, for my children, but other than that, I felt completely lost and overwhelmed.

My phone started to ring. News of Michael's death was spreading. The first call was from James, Michael's business partner.

"Hey, Suzanne, I'm going to send a car up there for you so you can come home," James said when I answered the phone.

That was the first thing he said. Not "Oh my god! I lost my partner," or "I'm so sorry," or "Is there anything I can do for you?"

Send a car for me? I was in Vermont. Three hours from home. I told him, "I'm not coming home tonight."

"Are you sure?" he asked.

"Yeah," I said and hung up.

My phone rang again. This time, it was William, our lawyer. Again, instead of words of comfort, he said, "I'll send a car."

"That's okay, William. I don't need one."

"C'mon, Suzanne," he pressed. "I'll come up and get you."

"William, I'm just not ready yet."

William sounded strange. Like James. There was desperation in his voice, not concern.

William wouldn't take no for an answer, and the back-and-forth continued until finally my friend Evelyn, one of the skating moms, took the phone and said, "Look, she'll come home when she's ready," and clicked off the call.

What was that about? I wondered. I knew I had to get my wits about me. And I had vowed to myself that I would not take any medication—not even an aspirin—or drink alcohol until I figured out what to do. Not that I was a big medication taker or drinker anyway, but I needed to be fully cognizant of what was happening.

The next day, Evelyn drove Ally and me back to Massachusetts, and when we pulled into the driveway, sure enough, William and his wife, Mary Ellen, were right there waiting for us. Evelyn had become a good friend and offered to stay with me.

"Are you all right?" William said as they walked in with us. Still, neither of them had said how sorry they were about Michael. That spoke volumes. After a few pleasantries, my daughter and Evelyn's daughter went upstairs to her bedroom. Then the talk turned serious.

"We need to get all your financials together," William said. "And we need you to sign some papers."

I couldn't understand the urgency. I was still trying to get used to the idea of standing in my home—the home I had bought with my husband—without him around. There was a looming absence. Like a missing appendage. I wondered if that feeling would ever go away. When I finally got a minute to myself away from them, Evelyn whispered, "This doesn't smell right, Suzanne."

Little did I know how right she was.

* * *

"Remember, Mom: Don't trust James," Ally reminded me. Ally and I were driving in Boston one morning, and she was telling me how she and Michael had gone out for ice cream recently, and he told her, "If anything ever happens to me, make sure you tell Mom not to trust James."

Ally's words weren't news to me. It wasn't like the hairs on my arms stood up or anything. I had known for a long time that Michael didn't trust his business partner, James. I didn't know why exactly, but I knew enough. For example, about a year before Michael's death, James wanted to take out loans for our three dealerships—Pride Hyundai, Pride Kia, and Pride Chevy—for renovations. After a certain number of years, car manufacturers want you to refurbish your dealership to change with the times—new colors, new furniture, a new outside facade. The three loans totaled around $7 million. That's a lot of money, even for a successful business.

Michael wasn't happy about it and wanted to renovate only one dealership at a time, which meant one loan. He didn't want a lot of debt since the dealerships never had mortgages. When Michael's parents owned and operated Pride, they never owed anyone, so Michael wanted to keep the borrowing to a minimum.

Still, James pushed to do all three loans and borrow all $7

million at the same time. Somehow, James got his way. One day, when the contractor who was supposed to be doing our Chevy renovation didn't show up at the job, Michael asked, "Where are the builders?" We found out they were at James's house, installing a pool and pool house in his backyard. All on Pride's dime.

That was all I knew, but I knew James could be sneaky. And I had a feeling that was just the tip of the iceberg.

People often asked me why Michael would make someone a business partner if he didn't trust that person. That's a good question. And I don't know the answer—Michael didn't discuss his work with me—but James had worked for my father-in-law. He had been the general manager for years. He knew the business, so there wouldn't have been a learning curve if Michael had brought him on board as partner. That was important at the time because Michael was starting to lose interest in the business.

When Michael's parents died (his mother in 2007 and his father in 2009), Michael's passion for the dealership died with them. They had always worked as a team. I believe my husband made James a partner because he had no desire to be in the car business anymore, and this was a way to slowly ease out of it.

Bringing James on board appeared to have been a quick decision. The initial partnership agreement between them was written on a napkin—very casual and lacking any real legal standing. They eventually signed official contracts, but William, who had no real experience in car business law, drew them up, so Michael and James's relationship didn't start off on solid footing.

If I had any chance of taking over the dealership, I knew I would have to disassociate myself from James. What I didn't know was that I would have to disassociate myself from William too.

* * *

Over the next few days, William was at my house every day, saying, "Okay, this is what we have to do next."

He would say, "Well, James wants to be there when you go and pick out the casket and when you pay for the funeral. He's nice enough that he's going to pay for it," which, I knew even then, was bullshit. My husband's business partner wasn't paying for the funeral. Pride Motor Group, my estate, was paying for Michael's funeral. But at the time, William wanted me to think that James was doing this out of the goodness of his heart.

The two of them continued to tag team me. If William wasn't singing James's praises, James was calling and saying things like, "Make sure you're not putting him in the most expensive casket," or "Take it easy on the flowers." I couldn't believe he was telling me what I could and couldn't do for my husband's arrangements. I felt surrounded. If I had to run errands, William was there. If I had to get my hair colored, his wife, Mary Ellen, was there. If the phone rang, it was James. The only time I was by myself was when I went home to bed.

There were reasons they were being so nice. Mary Ellen was getting a brand-new Suburban, and Pride Motor Group was paying for it. James was going to give William more money if they could get me to sign the paperwork that essentially cut me out of the business. I found all this out later. Apparently, William and Mary Ellen weren't shy about telling the world of their plans, and friends of mine what they were up to at a Halloween party.

At the time, though, I was clueless. William had me looking for all kinds of paperwork throughout the house—something that Michael had drawn up that showed that James was the sole owner of the dealerships upon Michael's death. (Michael and I had talked about doing a will, but we never got around to it, even though we had everything in place.) I was pretty sure that there was nothing like that around. After all, Michael had told Ally not to trust James. Why would he bequeath the business to him upon his death? It didn't make sense.

But I continued to look because at the time, I thought only James was untrustworthy. I didn't know that William was too. I had been friends with Mary Ellen for so long. We had mutual friends. She was like a sister to me. I could never dream she would do anything to hurt me or my family.

But greed often prevails.

I gave them whatever they wanted—bank statements, financial documents, etc. I even took William to the bank to look at my safety deposit box, just in case this will was in there. When I opened the box, I found a bunch of elastics, all broken, so at one point, I guess, Michael must have had a lot of money in there. When William saw the broken rubber bands, his face fell. No documentation. No money.

There *was* one thing in there, though—a ring Michael had worn in high school. Thinking it was a nice gesture, I gave it to William.

"Why don't you take this as a remembrance of Michael?" I said.

William's face was priceless. I could almost hear him thinking, *This is another dead end.*

That was when things started to click for me. Right there, in the safety deposit box viewing room. I could feel it. The tension. The disappointment. Maybe because the room was so small. I knew something was up, but who thinks that people want to screw you? Especially in the wake of the most devastating event of your life.

* * *

Michael and James had been talking about getting another business partner and opening a Chrysler-Dodge-Jeep dealership. I didn't know much about it. All I had to go on were bits and pieces that Michael told me in passing. He never wanted to bring his work home with him, which is commendable, but I knew virtually nothing about what was going on with him professionally. And since he had been going into the office less and less, I never really had a reason to ask questions.

But one day, out of the blue, not long before he was killed, he had someone come to the house and measure him for suits.

"I have to go back to work for a while," Michael told me. "I really don't want to, but James and I want to get more dealerships."

"Why would you want to get more dealerships when you don't want to be at the ones you have?" I asked.

He never really answered, and what struck me as strange was that while the Pride dealerships were located on the Lynnway in Lynn, thirty minutes south from my house, the Chrysler-Dodge-Jeep dealership was thirty minutes the other way. But I just accepted that all this was a positive sign that Michael was going to snap out of his funk and be more involved with the business. And hopefully with our family.

What I didn't know was that Michael hadn't signed any paperwork for that new dealership. He was supposed to—the day after he was killed. I also didn't know that James had bad blood with Chrysler, Dodge, and Jeep, and the manufacturer would only approve the deal if my husband was involved. Without Michael, James was stuck.

That was where I came in.

As a principal of the Pride dealerships, I could sign in Michael's stead.

But why would I? I was trying to break ties with James. It didn't matter, though. James never asked me to.

Instead, Doug, one of my husband's general managers, *forged my husband's signature.*

That was how, I found out later, James was able to buy the Chrysler-Dodge-Jeep dealership under the Iovanna name.

Illegally.

And to make matters worse, for this particular transaction, James had 40 percent ownership, which meant that James now had:

- 10 percent ownership of Pride Hyundai and Pride Kia
- 20 percent ownership of Pride Chevy
- 40 percent ownership of this new Chrysler-Dodge-Jeep dealership

Why was it so important to James to bring another dealership into the mix? Because he wanted more money.

Of course, I didn't know any of this at first. When I refused to sign the paperwork, I thought that was it. I thought James had contracted with Chrysler-Dodge-Jeep on his own.

I went about my business. Through the end of 2014 and much of 2015, I didn't go into the dealerships at all. I thought that could wait. I thought the business could sustain itself while I figured things out at home. I had so much on my plate with the estate attorney, settling my son into college, and helping my daughter, who had parted ways with her skating partner. I was traveling back and forth to Europe, just trying to find a new normal for my family.

All that time, I knew James was up to something with the new dealership, but I thought that was his business, and I was under the impression that everything was under control at Pride Motor Group. I thought the company bills were being paid, and I thought my personal bills were being paid, since my husband always had his secretary, Laurel, pay them from our personal trust. I thought the business was thriving and profitable.

I thought wrong.

Instead, it was a financial bloodbath with an attempted takeover.

Instead of taking a year off after my husband's death, I should have been at the dealership the very next day.

* * *

My husband's secretary, Laurel, did all the banking for the company, and she also handled our personal finances. Every month, Michael would say to me, "Oh, give me the bills for the houses, and I'll have Laurel pay them." We had our own checking account through Iovanna Realty—a trust that my in-laws had established in the 1980s. For years, Michael took Laurel the invoices for the mortgage and other bills, and she paid them.

The week before Michael died, I gave him the bills and just assumed that they were all paid. Over time, my mailbox at home became flooded with late payment notices.

I called James asking about it, but my calls went unreturned. Finally, I called Laurel directly, and she said, "Suzanne, I'm sorry. James told me not to pay any of those."

What? Lack of payment was ruining my credit. I immediately thought of my husband and how he used to tease me about my FICO credit score because mine was a perfect 850, and his was two down from me.

"How am I not perfect?" he would say. "I pay the bills, and *my* name is on everything." "I don't know," I'd say. And I didn't. (I had—and still have—no idea how that works.) I asked Laurel why James would do that, but she said she didn't know.

But I knew. James wanted to screw up my books. Mess with my financial reputation. "I'm really sorry," said Laurel, who was also working for James's other dealership. "He made me do it. What can I do to help?"

I decided right there and then that, when I took over the business, I would fill the dealership with honest employees. Laurel would be the first person I let go.

Chapter 7

SUZANNE, DETECTIVE

ON THANKSGIVING DAY 2014, WHILE MOST PEOPLE WERE sitting down with their families and enjoying a meal, I was spying on my business partner.

Mikey and I drove to the new Chrysler-Dodge-Jeep dealership—the one I'd assumed James had bought on his own when I wouldn't sign the paperwork. But I had a nagging feeling that something wasn't right.

When we pulled up, we saw a big sign that read, *Excuse Our Appearance*, with five cars parked in what looked like a used car lot. There were no car photos up yet and just a makeshift logo that read, *This Is Pride*.

Pride? I thought, surprised.

I said to my son, "Are those our cars?"

"Let's get out and see," he said.

We did, and sure enough, they *were* our cars. James was selling Pride automobiles from a dealership that, as far as I was concerned, was not Pride.

Mikey began taking photos of all the VIN numbers. "Good," I said. This was the proof I needed. This would show my lawyer that James was up to no good. This would be what I needed to finally break ties with him altogether.

Later that week, I showed our photos to my lawyer, William. "Oh, James just had to borrow them," he said. "He's not really selling them there. You just don't understand."

I knew he was gaslighting me. I wasn't going to fall for it.

I *knew* James was selling my cars out of that dealership, so I schemed up a plan. I had one of my friends go with his son and pretend to buy a car. Sure enough, when my friend walked in, the salesperson tried to sell him one of my cars, but he knew enough not to let my friend test drive the car off the property, which would have been illegal. "You can drive around the parking lot, if you like," the salesperson said.

I didn't know what to do.

But I knew William had to go. I had had enough.

At Michael's funeral, I had chatted with my son's high school hockey coach, who was also a very close friend and someone I knew I could trust.

"Do you think you can help me find an automotive lawyer?" I had asked.

He knew what I was up against. He had sized up James and William immediately and knew I was getting screwed. "Suzanne," he said, "they're going to continue taking advantage of you. You need to find somebody *fast*."

A friend of his put me in touch with a lawyer named Benjamin, who represented a lot of dealers in the area. I was elated. I finally had a lawyer I could trust.

Meanwhile, William continued to hound me. "C'mon, Suzanne, you need to sign this, do that, do this."

"You know what, William?" I said finally. "Okay, let's meet for lunch."

I woke up that morning excited for the first time in a

long time. Firing James would give me my power back. I met William in a nearby Qdoba, and no sooner had we sat down than William began pulling papers from his briefcase and spreading them out across the table. I stopped him before he could say a word. I knew exactly what I was going to say, and I felt confident.

"You know what, William? I just don't feel good about this whole thing. Something about this…in my stomach…doesn't feel right. And I know, deep in your heart, you would never want to hurt me or my two children."

I stopped here to see his reaction. He had none. People without a conscience tend not to.

"I know this because my husband did a lot for you." I looked at all the papers in front of me. "That being said, this kind of thing, automotive law, is not in your wheelhouse, so not only am I *not* going to sign the papers, but I've hired another lawyer who is an expert in automotives."

His face dropped.

Up until that moment, he thought I would *finally* sign the paperwork that would give James full control of Pride. Instead, I fired him.

It was one of the best days of my life.

But just the beginning of the rest of the whole nightmare.

* * *

If James was selling my cars on the new dealership's lot, I began to wonder what else he was doing that I needed to know about.

I went spying again after New Year's Day 2015 and found out something new. Not only was the new dealership selling my cars, but my employees were working there too!

They were working for James, and I was paying them. I'm sure they didn't know what was going on. Their paychecks said *Pride Chevrolet* or *Pride*, and the new dealership's *Pardon Our Appearance* sign had been replaced with a great big new sign, in the same font as Pride, that read: *Pride Chrysler-Dodge-Jeep*. They thought they were dealing with the same company.

But James knew what was going on.

And to make matters worse, I also found out that *my* dealerships had bought some of James's Jeeps, and James had placed them at my Chevy dealership. He had called up every one of my vendors and said, "Hey, Pride's getting a new dealership. Send the bills for this new dealership over to Pride."

I was paying millions of dollars for that dealership to get started.

A dealership that wasn't mine.

I began sending all my reconnaissance work—photos, documentation—to my new lawyer, Benjamin, asking, "Can we do anything? I know James is stealing and committing other crimes. What position am I in?"

It was a question that I never asked William. I never got the chance. William always told me, "James is doing you a favor by letting you stay and giving you a job, and you should be grateful." William would say, "Don't worry. Running a dealership is hard. James will take care of you. I spoke to James, and he told me, 'I loved Michael. Michael gave me this opportunity. It's the least I can do.'"

Finally, I had a lawyer in the automotive industry. A lawyer with new insights. A new perspective.

Unfortunately, my new lawyer, Benjamin, started giving me the same song and dance. "Why don't you try working *with* James?" Benjamin said. "This could be a positive thing."

What? Benjamin was trying to get me to work with James too? "Even with everything that is going on?" I asked. "I know James wants to take Pride away from me."

"Oh, don't worry about it," Benjamin said. "He can't do that much."

I pushed and pushed. I knew something was wrong. And that something had to be done. What I didn't know was that Benjamin and James's lawyer had once worked together, which created a conflict of interest. That meant Benjamin couldn't be impartial, and he didn't have *my* best interests at heart.

"Fine," Benjamin said finally after my continued prodding. "I'll draw up the cease-and-desist letter."

Whew. At least that's something, I thought. We would send a cease and desist to James, and he would have to stop selling my cars and taking my people. I felt a bit better as my daughter and I prepared to travel to North Carolina for one of her skating competitions.

To his credit, Benjamin did draw up the cease and desist. And I paid him for his time in writing it.

He just never sent it.

Who knows why.

Maybe he was in cahoots with James's lawyer. Maybe he saw me as a widow he could take advantage of. Maybe he simply forgot.

I don't know. But I went off to North Carolina thinking that things were finally in motion and that the right thing was going to be done.

But they weren't.

Nothing had changed when I returned.

Benjamin kept telling me, "Don't worry about the new dealership. James has no money. He can't do anything."

That wasn't true. James had money. He had my husband's money. And he was spending it like water.

"He's not going to be able to get that dealership running, Suzanne," Benjamin told me. "I don't know," I said. "He knows a lot of people. What if he gets a partner?"

"Don't worry about it. He won't." He did.

* * *

The Lynnway serves as the main artery of Lynn, Massachusetts—a north-south connection within, to, and from the city that is heavily trafficked and loaded with businesses, especially automotive businesses like AutoZone, Jiffy Lube, and a bunch of car dealerships.

When my father-in-law was still alive, a guy named Jack Stone owned a car dealership across the street from his Chevy dealership on the Lynnway, but Jack later sold it and turned it into a store that he rented out. Jack had bought up most of the Lynnway—my father-in-law was always outbid by this guy by, like, a dollar or a quarter. They didn't get along.

Jack got to know James when James was my father-in-law's general manager. He agreed to become James's partner on the new dealership, but there was a catch: He wasn't going to put in a dime. Instead, Jack said, "You'd better get everything out of *her* that you can." I know this because my general manager told me, and I also saw the invoices when I later became more involved in the business.

At the time, Pride needed an extra lot—more space to store my vehicles. Michael had been renting the land behind Jack's store, where he had an office. After Michael died, I continued using that lot because I really needed the space.

And Jack *knew* I needed the space.

Before Michael died, Pride was paying $2,000 a month in rent.

After Michael died, Jack doubled the rent to $4,000 a month.

Then, when James and Jack became partners, he charged $6,000 a month—essentially extorting me to pay, in part, for this new dealership.

They were taking my money. My employees. And my vendors. James and Jack walked into that dealership paying for virtually nothing.

I tried to prove all this stuff and contact my lawyer but got nowhere. I was getting screwed. Again. I felt defeated.

And I was about to be sued.

Chapter 8

SUZANNE, DEFENDANT

REMEMBER GWEN? THE FRIEND I CALLED WHEN I believed Michael had been killed? Well, she was suing me for $20 million.

I had met Gwen and her husband, Samuel, through Michael—they all hung out with the Harley-Davidson motorcycle crowd. Samuel and Gwen were about ten years younger than we were and had a daughter, Hazel, who was the same age as Ally.

"I met this really nice couple," Michael told me. "You'll love Gwen. I want you to meet them."

We started going out for dinner and hit it off. I really, really liked Samuel. He was like me, a Mr. Mom. He got up in the morning, got the kids situated and dressed, made their lunches, and took them to school. Gwen, on the other hand, seemed to be a bit of a prima donna—always had her nails done, worked out, tended to sleep in. There's nothing wrong with that, of course, but we just weren't all that compatible. I liked her, but I knew immediately that she would never be one of my besties.

Samuel's parents used to own a convenience store, and he ended up scratching a multimillion-dollar ticket. After that, he basically retired. He and Gwen bought three family homes, and he became the maintenance guy—Mr. Fix-It as well as Mr. Mom. If a pipe burst, he was on it. He was really good with his hands. Gwen, on the other hand, was more of the manager. She was the one at home saying, "Hey, go collect the rent. They owe us $1,200." She was the bank and ran the books.

Samuel and Michael became very close friends because Michael was essentially semiretired too. With James as his partner, and as the kids got older, he could party or sit at home during the day and not have any stress. Like Samuel, he had a lot of time on his hands.

The four of us became a tight unit. We went to each other's homes. They had parties. We had parties. Samuel and Michael became inseparable—Gwen too. They were like the Three Musketeers. They did everything together, while I was busy with the kids. My son was driving by now and could fend for himself, but Ally was homeschooled, and I took her skating first thing every morning. I dropped her off at 8:00 a.m., came back home, got the house in order, did food shopping, played a little tennis, and then went back and picked her up. With the hours on the road in Boston traffic and her other figure skating activities, shuttling Ally around was a full-time job.

Two months prior to Michael's and Samuel's deaths, Samuel and Gwen and their girls came to our Cape house, and our two families took our boat to Nantucket for a really nice weekend. Our girls got along well enough, and because Ally was skating a lot of the time, most of her friends were from different parts of Massachusetts. She wasn't close to anyone from our town because she was homeschooled, so she enjoyed the time spent with Hazel.

Two weeks prior to Michael's and Samuel's deaths, the four of us went to Boston's North End, an Italian neighborhood with lots of restaurants and bakeries, for one of the area's popular feasts. I mentioned that I had to take Ally to a skating competition in Vermont in a couple of weeks.

"I'm kind of worried," I said to Samuel and Gwen. "You know how Michael doesn't like to be left alone."

Michael was drinking again—he had toned it down, but it was starting to pick up, and my kids and I were ready to have an intervention once my son came home from Canada. Samuel and Gwen said not to worry, that they would take care of him, and that I should go and have fun.

The day before the accident, while Ally and I were in Vermont, Gwen and Samuel texted me and sent pictures of where the three of them went for dinner, letting me know that Michael was home and that everything was okay. When I talked to Michael about four hours before the accident—the conversation that ended without Ally saying she loved him—he seemed sober, and everything seemed great. However, I found out from a friend that Michael, Samuel, and Gwen had gone to an Italian restaurant the night before and then wound up at a Chinese restaurant, where Michael had gotten so inebriated that somebody had to drive him home.

The signs were all there. His drinking was getting out of control. But when I spoke to Gwen the night of Michael's death, she downplayed it, saying she had just seen him and that she was sure he and Samuel were fine.

As we know, she was wrong.

Michael's wake and funeral came and went. So did Samuel's. I didn't go to Samuel's, and Gwen didn't come to Michael's. I wanted to go to Samuel's, but I received legal advice that it wasn't a good idea. I'm sure Gwen got the same advice.

About two months later, I had to take Ally to a skating competition in North Carolina, and I received an email while we were getting our bags off the conveyor belt at the airport baggage claim that Gwen was suing me for $20 million. It wasn't a *complete* surprise. Gwen and I had mutual friends, and I had a feeling that something was in the works.

Why $20 million? That was how much all three Pride properties were insured for. Michael had just increased the value. If the lawsuit had happened two months prior, Gwen probably wouldn't have sought that much.

Of course, I panicked. I reached out to the guy my friend had recommended, the one who had put me in touch with Benjamin. He told me to calm down and try to think clearly, but it was hard. I understood that Gwen had lost her husband, but I was so hurt by her betrayal. I thought we were friends. We both had husbands who died and children to take care of. I thought maybe she would say, "Listen, I'm going to have to go after you. Let's work this out." But that's not how it went down. Instead, she blamed my daughter and me for Samuel's death, saying that I *killed* her husband because Michael didn't come with us to the skating competition.

Killed her husband?

Michael *never* went on those skating trips. That really stung.

And all those friends in the Harley-Davidson group that Michael was a part of? None of them stood by me. They all chose Gwen. Also, with Michael gone, they lost their meal ticket. My husband tended to pay for everybody all the time. Now that he was gone, who would buy the beers? Who would pick up the tab? I don't think any of those people were ever really Michael's friends. Except Samuel.

If being sued weren't bad enough, as part of the lawsuit,

I was required to watch footage of Michael at a local bar to see what transpired prior to his and Samuel's deaths.

I watched every tape. I watched my husband order three vodka tonics. And because Michael and Samuel were regulars, the bartender knew that Michael tipped very well, so when she poured a drink, she double-poured. He had three doubles, which was really six drinks, and Samuel had two.

I know this sounds like a lot of booze for one person, but this was over a four-hour period. And Michael also had something to eat. A sandwich or something. Not that I'm making excuses for him. He had been drinking. A lot.

But there was another problem. Michael took Ambien at night to sleep, and it was still in his system from the night before. The Ambien enhanced Michael's alcohol level—or at least that was what they told me.

They also told me that Michael had driven his Porsche Cayenne to the bar, while Samuel had driven his Mercedes. They drove both those cars back to my house, which seemed weird to me. I don't think Samuel was intoxicated at all. Was Michael? The coroner said yes. I argued that the fact that Michael was able to drive from the restaurant to my house, which is probably six miles, without getting into an accident or realizing he was intoxicated was proof that he was stable. But they said that because Michael was so familiar with the route, his body simply went into memory mode, and he was able to drive home without a problem.

I didn't buy it. *How could he do that? How could he stay home for an hour and a half, go running after my dog, and then get into the Ferrari drunk?* I would have bet my life that something had gone wrong with the car, since at that time the model was having trouble, and *that* caused the accident. It didn't make sense.

Still, one of my neighbors had spoken to them that night when the dog had gotten loose and reported that Michael was under the influence and that Samuel wasn't. And then once they took the dog home and got into the car, they stopped at the end of the street (there were only ten homes on the street) to talk to another neighbor—a framer, someone who had built the homes in the area. When my lawyer contacted him to ask if he thought Michael was drunk, he said yes.

Two neighbors believed Michael was drunk. And yet Michael's friend, Samuel, was right there with him. Couldn't he, too, see that Michael was drunk? Samuel's car was parked right at my home. Why didn't they get into Samuel's car? Why didn't Samuel drive? Why did they take the Ferrari? Why didn't Samuel say, "Let me drive"? Samuel wasn't one to let someone drive drunk.

There were so many unanswered questions. I knew what the coroner said. I knew what my neighbors testified. And I also knew that Michael's drinking had become a problem again. But I also knew in my heart that Michael would never have gotten into that Ferrari if he had been drunk.

My lawyer said, "Well, why can't Suzanne sue the bar for overserving her husband?" This wasn't the bar's first lawsuit. Someone else had died after being overserved. Gwen's lawyer, who initially said he was only going after Pride, wound up suing Pride *and* the bar for overserving Michael. (She had a really good lawyer.) In the end, Gwen was awarded $15 million from the Iovanna estate and the bar. I received a settlement of about $75,000 from the bar.

After that court appearance, I never saw Gwen again.

Well, at least not until we met up at a police station a year later.

                              * * *

Ally got a new skating partner, Paolo, and after they trained
and competed together in the States, we traveled to Europe
for more competitions. When we were in Estonia, Paolo
dropped Ally during competition, and she landed on her
head and got a concussion. Her coach thought it would be
best if we came home the next day so that Ally could see the
doctors in Boston.

About two weeks after we arrived home, Ally got *another*
concussion. We were driving into Boston one day, and the sun
was very bright on the highway. Traffic had come almost to
a stop. A kid was on his phone in the car behind us, texting.
He never saw the cars slowing down, so he came crashing
into me.

That marked the end of Ally's skating career.

She became bedridden after the second concussion since
her brain hadn't healed yet from the first. She had to stay in
bed for months, and then she got headaches and was dizzy
when she tried to skate again.

There would be another big change for her. For most of
her life, Ally was homeschooled. This allowed her to train
in the morning when there weren't a lot of skaters on the ice.
Now that skating was over, she decided she wanted to spend
her senior year in school with other students, so we enrolled
her in the district public high school.

She thrived immediately.

Ally made the cheer squad team, and during the competitions, the team had pasta parties at the cheerleaders' houses.
I volunteered to have the first one. I wanted to meet the girls.
I wanted to meet their moms because some of them I hadn't
seen since the girls were little, and some I didn't know. We

had a great time. Ally was on cloud nine. She was busy. She was making friends and making a new life for herself. I was so happy that after Michael's death we could try to find some normalcy again.

I didn't attend the next pasta party, and Ally wound up calling me, crying hysterically. I couldn't understand what she was saying and told her to calm down. She explained that all the girls were sitting around and eating when their phones went off, and they all started receiving the same types of messages:

I can't believe you're with a killer.

She killed my dad.

How do you girls even look at yourself facing that Iovanna?

The messages were from Gwen's daughter Hazel. Even though she lived in the next town, she knew the girls through cheerleading and dance. She and Ally may have been good friends while their fathers were alive, but after Samuel died, Hazel turned.

Listen, I get it.

Her dad died. And he was the rock of her family.

But *we* didn't tell Michael to drive the car. Ally and I had nothing to do with it. I loved Samuel.

Ally's friends told her, "Don't worry. Relax," but Ally was so upset. The harassment didn't stop there.

Hazel started showing up wherever my daughter was. If Ally was at the ice cream parlor with friends, they'd see Hazel stalking them. If my daughter and her friends went to the mall, to a dance, or got their makeup done, Hazel was there.

And she was writing horrible things about Ally on the internet—basically, more of what she had written in the text messages.

"Just block her," I told Ally. "Whatever she posts, who gives a flying poop?" But it got really bad—especially when Hazel got the police involved.

She told the local police department that Ally and her friend Amanda ran her off the road. Police officers went to Ally's school looking for them, and when they couldn't find them, they showed up at Amanda's house. When Ally discovered what Hazel had told them, she said that she and Amanda weren't even around at that time—they were in Florida. She even provided proof to the officer, who also worked as a security guard at Ally's school. She explained that it was Hazel who was harassing *her*. Not the other way around.

Still, the police took Hazel's charges seriously. All I could think was, *Wow, all those years of homeschooling and skating—that was so much easier. I escaped the drama!*

I was upset with Hazel but also felt so bad for her. She was struggling with the loss of her dad. I had heard that Gwen had a boyfriend and thought maybe that was why Hazel was lashing out, but I wasn't sure.

I went to the local police department to try to straighten things out. Or at least provide our side of the story. "I know it's hard," the officer said, "but you're just going to have to write down all the things Hazel is doing and when all these events take place, and you're going to have to build a case."

"Can you at least give her a restraining order?" I asked. "My daughter doesn't go to Hazel's town. My daughter doesn't go to any town Hazel is near. It's not like she's trying to find her."

The officer agreed to a two-week restraining order.

That two-week period after the police station visit was wonderful. Hazel didn't post anything on social media. The harassment stopped.

Then we had to return to court to get a permanent restraining order. My daughter was a nervous wreck. My lawyer, Clara (you'll learn about her in a bit—she's Lawyer #3), couldn't make it but said, "I don't have to be there. This is a slam dunk. They should give it to you. Don't worry. I'm sure the judge will see that the problem is Hazel, not Ally."

But that wasn't the case.

When we got to the courthouse, Hazel strutted in like a lawyer with a big folder of files and paperwork, along with Gwen, Gwen's boyfriend, and a lawyer, like it was some sort of corporate takeover. It felt like *Jerry Springer*.

"Mom, what's going on?" Ally asked me nervously. "It'll be all right," I said. I was anxious.

The judge called Ally up to the bench and asked her to plead her case. Poor Ally. She was so nervous and very emotional, so she left out a lot of her talking points. But when Hazel approached the bench, she was totally on point. What a performance! She could have won a Golden Globe.

In the end, the judge brought us all up to the bench and told us that he had two daughters and that granting the permanent restraining order would affect Hazel for the rest of her life and go on her permanent record, and he felt that wouldn't be fair. I didn't care about Hazel's permanent record. I just wanted the harassment to stop.

In the end, we didn't get the restraining order, but the judge did say that Hazel needed to leave Ally alone and stay away from her.

And she did.

For two weeks.

Then she was at it again.

At that point, I knew that we just had to suck it up.

"Ally, there's nothing we can do," I said. "Our hands are

tied. You'll be starting college soon, so who cares? Hazel's going to North Carolina. You're going to Connecticut."

Fortunately, that was what happened. It all worked out in the end, but Hazel was relentless until the day she left.

And with that behind us, I could focus on getting the car dealerships under control and reclaiming my Pride.

Chapter 9

SUZANNE, RECRUIT

IN 2014 AND 2015, I SPENT A MILLION DOLLARS ON lawyers who didn't have my best interests at heart. People always ask me why I didn't sue James, how I let him get away with forging my husband's name on documentation and using my cars and employees for a dealership that I had no connection to. The truth was that I didn't know I could! I had two lawyers, William and then Benjamin, working on my behalf, or so I thought, and neither one suggested that I had rights. If I had known, I could have sued James for stealing, which, at the very least, meant that the manufacturers wouldn't let him run the dealerships.

Around August 2015, a friend who was like a second dad to Michael said to me, "Look, I really don't think that this Benjamin guy is helping you. First of all, he should have sent a cease-and-desist order to James right away. It's ludicrous! You spent a million dollars on what? What have you gotten? James is still there, and he's still probably stealing from you."

He was right. "My cousin is a lawyer," he said. "Maybe she can help."

I switched lawyers immediately, telling Benjamin his services were no longer needed. Clara wasn't an automotive lawyer, and she didn't know about the business, so I had that problem again, but I hoped things would be different. When I first met her, Clara was gung-ho about nabbing James, but then when I hired her, she began to backtrack. "Well, I don't know how much we can do. The manufacturers will want to take your dealerships."

Oh, no, I thought. Was this Benjamin all over again?

I didn't have time to look for another lawyer. I needed to get on top of the business. I had been away for too long—dealing with the estate, with Gwen, with Ally—and I knew my finances weren't pretty. That first year after Michael's death, I was just so mad at everybody.

Mad at Michael for getting me in this place.

Mad at my lawyers for screwing me.

Mad at James for screwing me.

That whole year was just anger.

I had been so naive. Yes, I had problems with my family growing up, but at least I grew up with people I trusted. I didn't have to watch my back all the time. People weren't always trying to take things from me—I didn't have anything to take, I guess, at the time. I had never dealt with those types of people before. It was a lot to face, and it wasn't fun.

But I made a decision to move forward. Going into the latter half of 2015 and into 2016 and beyond, there would be no more looking back. I had no choice. I had two children to take care of, and I was scared, overwhelmed, and angry. I was going to seize whatever opportunities I could and make pink lemonade out of the pile of lemons I had been given. Plus, I wanted to show my kids I could do this.

One night, I was in the billiard room in my house, which

was the room I felt most comfortable in for some reason, and the phone rang. It was Clara.

"Have you been to the dealership yet?" she asked.

"No," I said. The estate and my kids had been taking up so much of my time.

"Well, I suggest that you get in there, because God only knows what's been going on this year."

"Well, I can already tell you that I invested in a dealership that I don't own."

"Okay," Clara said. "You have to start making a presence. You have to take these dealerships back. We need to figure out what's going on. I have an idea."

"What?"

"You should have a pizza party."

"A pizza party?"

"Yeah. Go to the dealership and introduce yourself. Bring a pizza. Everybody loves pizza."

I didn't think it would be that easy. In fact, I knew it wouldn't be. I had been out of work for fifteen years raising my children. And I didn't know how to be a boss. I'd always *had* a boss. How could I just go in there and expect to be treated like a boss when I wasn't exactly sure what a boss was supposed to do?

At the time, my husband's cousin Joe had been in touch with me. I told him how nervous I was, and he said, "Look, you don't want to go in there alone. I'll go with you—not to do a good cop-bad cop thing, but maybe they'll take you a little more seriously if I come with you. I'll drive you in the first day."

I knew this was a good idea immediately. A lot of the employees knew that Joe was Michael's cousin, and he would give the impression *You screw with her, you're gonna deal with me.* Also, it's no secret that the car business is a man's world. Women in the automotive industry are few and far between. If I wanted to get my foot in the door, I needed a wingman.

One day in September 2015, Joe picked me up from my house, and we drove to my Chevy dealership. When we got there, I walked around and checked out the service department, the sales department, and the office (I decided to have the pizza party another day). I went around to every employee and introduced myself. "I don't know what you've been told, and I'm sorry I haven't been here, but I'm going to be working here now."

All this got back to James, who was outraged. "What is she doing here?" I could hear him yelling.

Joe was adamant. "You're going to go into your husband's office, and you're going to sit there, and you're just not going to leave."

And that's how I got started at Pride. I started coming into the office every morning. The employees set me up with a computer, but I didn't know a thing about technology—and I knew even less about the car business. There were so many acronyms and terms. I mean, I'm used to acronyms in the dental world, but this was different.

"You need to start going to meetings," Clara told me. "Even though you might not know what the hell they're talking about, you need to be present. That's how you'll start to show people *Oh, she isn't just a widow.*"

I took her advice. Every day, I forced myself to attend whatever meetings. James would look at me like *What the hell are you doing here?* But I had every right to be there, so I stayed, even though he undermined me every step of the way. When I asked him questions directly, he either didn't answer or said something that I knew was a lie. Or he might say something wonderfully supportive like "Suzanne, I want to work with you. I'll do anything for you." And then when I wasn't around, he would tell my staff, "If she asks you any questions, report to me. Do not tell her *anything*." He instructed the employees not to talk to me at all. Every day, I felt alone and out of my element—even though about a hundred fifty employees worked for me.

But I didn't care. I wanted to prove to them—and to myself—that I could do this.

I took notes at every meeting, even though I didn't know what the heck I was writing. Everything was way over my head and totally overwhelming. Front ends. Back ends. F&I. OEM. DSM. GSM. GM. It was like they were speaking Chinese. I understood nothing. I'm not saying if I had been younger that it would have been easier, but being forty-nine years old and not having worked in more than a decade made it that much harder.

But I stayed. I kept writing things down, terms I didn't know, things that I wasn't sure how to spell. I just kept writing, and then after each meeting I went to my desk, opened my computer, and looked everything up. I googled any word that I didn't understand. I wrote definition upon definition and studied them.

I was doing too much. Instead of saying to myself, *Okay, let me take aim at this department this week and that department the next*, I tried to learn everything at once, and it wasn't working. I was getting more and more frustrated. It had been about a year since my husband had died, and I felt like I was taking one step forward and three back.

But I was determined. If I had any hope of taking over this business, of changing the prevailing attitude and getting rid of

James, I knew I had to show that I was serious. And I thought if I did that, then maybe the employees would respond.

I continued going to the dealerships every day. I showed up at different times, so the employees never knew when to expect me. I worked seven days a week. Both of my children were busy with school, so it wasn't like I had anyone to go home to anyway—and with an almost empty nest, I found the job gave me purpose, even though I was in way over my head.

I could tell I was annoying people. Back then, dealerships were open until 9:00 at night, and I stayed late because I wanted to learn all I could, and I wanted to show my employees what real leadership looked like ("What? She's still here, and we can't close up yet?"). I also wanted to hold them accountable. Since my husband died, employees didn't show up, took long lunches, did whatever they wanted. That had to change.

But making a change was more difficult than I thought it would be. For the previous five years, James had run the show. Michael had put him in charge, so all hundred fifty employees, between all three dealerships, had been taking orders from him.

Michael only stopped by the dealership to give his secretary the bills and sign the checks. He would do a quick walk-around, and that was it, so any corporate culture had developed without Michael. Or me. There were a lot of moving parts that I needed to get to work together again.

Looking back, I really had no clue at the enormity of the task. Perhaps the only reason I was able to get through it was because I was so naive. I thought, *James is a jerk. Everyone will be happy to get rid of him, so once I get in here and buy him out, things will be different.*

James may have been a jerk, but he paid the employees (the ones he liked) really well, so they didn't mind doing his dirty work. The employees, by and large, were loyal to him—when someone is paying you a lot of money, you don't have much incentive to break ties.

What's more, when Michael was killed, it wasn't like James stepped it up. For more than a year, he hadn't worked much either. He was an absentee employer. But now that I was there, he had to work more. He didn't like that. In fact, he was beside himself. He thought getting rid of me was going to be easy-peasy lemon squeezy, but he underestimated me for too long. And I was biding my time. I knew I needed to hang in there, and the best way to do that was to learn the business.

* * *

Now that I was in the office every day, I was starting to figure out what I needed to do to get back control of Pride. First on my list: getting a handle on the finances. Which wasn't easy when the employees had been instructed not to talk to me. If I dared ask someone, "How do I find out about the bank deposits and finances?" I'd get the runaround. James could have been taking a million dollars out of the bank each day, and I didn't know.

I told Laurel, my husband's secretary (Remember her? The one who hadn't been paying my bills because James instructed her not to?), I needed the Iovanna Trust checkbook so I could pay my personal bills.

She looked at me like I had two heads. I'm sure the first thing she thought was, *I have to tell James!* She opened drawer after drawer looking for the checkbook, but her office was a disaster. I am very organized with my space, but Laurel was the opposite. Papers everywhere. I was getting the shakes watching her search.

Finally, she pulled it out of an overstuffed drawer. She handed it to me, and I told her confidently I was going to pay my bills from now on—even though I had no idea what I was doing.

I went into science and became a dental hygienist because I hated math. It's just not my forte. And because of that, I stayed away from anything math-related all my life if I could. It's embarrassing to say, but I never paid a bill, never bothered learning how to fill out a check. There was always somebody to do it for me. But now I was realizing that people were taking advantage of my lack of financial education. Like when I spent hours and hours in William's office complaining about James, and William made James out to be a good guy and invited me over to vent, like my therapist—"Oh, stay for lunch, and we'll chat!" All the while he was charging me for his time. *Cha-ching!* Well, the gravy train was ending. Suzanne was getting educated. But little did I know that figuring out how to balance a checkbook would be the easy part.

James was doing a lot of bad stuff. I already knew he was not above signing my husband's name on documents or encouraging others to do his bidding. But it went beyond that. He had more ownership in my Chevy dealership, and he changed the numbers to make them look better than the financials for Hyundai and Kia. This didn't just make me look like I was losing money hand over fist at Hyundai and Kia, but if Chevy was making more money, that meant James was making more money.

Also, he was stealing from the dealership's "metal money." Every month, we accumulate metal when we work on cars. The mechanics take out the old parts that don't work anymore, and we bring the parts that have metal in them—old rotors, etc.—to a scrap metal company that melts them down to reuse and gives us cash back for them.

Back then, the metal money was worth a lot, and James was probably stealing thousands of dollars every month. He told whatever employee he sent down to the scrap metal place to give him the cash instead of turning it in to the company. He was collecting a nice little stash! That may not sound like a lot of money, but when you're running a business, where monthly transactions are in the millions, these little thefts can really add up. The dealerships may have looked like they were thriving, but they were in the red and hemorrhaging badly. I knew I had to start making bigger changes. And because I was having so much trouble making changes from the inside, I decided to focus on the outside instead.

Chapter 10

SUZANNE, CHANGEMAKER

IN EARLY 2016, I DECIDED TO CHANGE MY ADVERTISING company. The one Michael and James had been using was now doing advertising for James's new dealership. And since that dealership was wrongfully using the Pride logo, there was nothing to distinguish us from them. I had to differentiate myself.

But I had another motive. Customers needed to see me as the new face of Pride. They needed to associate me with the company as they had Michael, who had been the spokesperson. Plus, it would be progressive to have a woman dealer principal in the spotlight, and I wanted Pride to move with the times.

But there was one problem: my anxiety. Did I really expect myself to go in front of a camera?

As nervous as I was, I told the executives of my new advertising firm, "I want to make a commercial. I know it's going to be difficult. I've never done a commercial before. I've never done speeches. But I need my customers to know that I'm representing Pride. I need them to know that Pride is Pride and that Pride is Kia, Hyundai, and Chevrolet."

The firm I hired worked with a lot of big companies, and the executives coached me on how to present myself on camera. I'll never forget that first day of shooting for our first commercial. The camera operators were on a dolly, and not only did I have to say my lines, but I had to say them while making sure I was looking at the camera. That meant I needed to talk slowly and clearly *and* walk at the same time.

This was *so* out of my wheelhouse. I didn't like being in the spotlight at all, so it was difficult, but I was so determined and so frustrated that I wasn't getting anywhere with the changes I wanted to make at the company. This was a chance to take my power back. Surprisingly, I had a knack for being on camera. I wasn't nervous at all. The director I worked with told me that normally he did a lot of retakes, but I did good first and second takes. He was impressed. "Wow, we work with the biggest car dealer in Massachusetts, and even *he* has a difficult time," the director said.

That made me feel even more relaxed and took the pressure off. I know that people like newscasters go to school to learn how to act, talk, and walk, but for some reason the performance came quickly to me. It's even easier now, seven years after my first commercial. I've done more than ten for each dealership.

When I look back at the ad spots Michael did, I can tell he was nervous: He had a weird smile on his face and didn't know where to look. Ironically, in real life, he was always the life of the party and didn't mind being the center of attention. I was the opposite. In real life, in crowds, I was the wallflower, but in front of the camera, I was a force. Go figure.

Maybe it's because while I'm shooting, I don't have a lot of people looking at me—only a director and a half dozen people doing lights and camera. I don't think about the thousands who are going to watch me later. (I was mortified, of course, when I saw that first commercial air on television.)

James had no idea that the new commercial was running or that I had changed advertising companies. Soon after I shot the commercial, I decided to have a big meeting and brought him and all the managers into one of the conference rooms. I said, "I'd like to introduce you to the new advertising agency I hired." I pointed to the owner of the company and asked her to introduce herself and talk about her firm. I said, "Then we're going to show you how we're changing the Pride Motor Group." I ran the commercial. And that was also when I introduced a new font for the Pride logo. For forty years, my in-laws and my husband had used the same font, but I had to make a change. James was using our font for his other dealership (still named Pride, by the way) and making it look like it belonged with our family of dealerships.

As the commercial ran, I could see that I was starting to get to James. After almost a year and a half of him taking advantage of me, I was finally taking a stand. (Little did I know that the old advertising agency was giving James a kickback. Finding a new advertising company meant cutting off some of his revenue.) I watched the faces of all the managers, all his minions. Their mouths were hanging open. They couldn't believe that I had fired their advertising agency and hired a new one.

It was one of the best days of my life. I was so proud of myself. It felt good to get out of my comfort zone. All that pent-up anger and disgust, all those months of feeling unheard, all that time that James had screwed me and hadn't even batted an eye was all behind me. I wasn't backing down. It felt like I was in a boxing match, and every time James or the employees thought I was down for the count, I kept popping back up.

And I was only getting started.

* * *

With the new advertising firm in place, I tackled the next item on my agenda.

Cleaning house.

If I could have, I would have fired just about everyone. But I couldn't. I still didn't know what I was doing. I needed people to help me run the company for now, so I had to bide my time. The first thing I did, though, was fire five or six employees who worked closely with James, including Laurel and my finance director, Rick, who was essentially James's second in command. Rick, who was making almost as much money as I was at the time, did not work every day and spent a lot of his time in James's dealership. When he *did* work, he tried to thwart my every move—giving me misinformation or no information—as I started to get more involved with vendors and the day-to-day business.

When I fired Rick, James went nuts. One by one, he was losing his minions. And things began to get even uglier. If that were possible.

James began treating me horribly. When he wasn't yelling, he was giving me the silent treatment—not interacting with me or telling me what was going on at the dealership. Meanwhile, when I went home, he would call and leave messages saying things like, "I'm not going to hurt you, Suzanne. You're going to make all the money. I loved Michael."

Yeah, sure.

Next, my lawyer Clara suggested I begin to sever internal

communications between all the company employees, which would keep them from trying to conspire against me and also from engaging in illegal activities. She hired a team to come in and take the manager's computer hard drives, which would prove that James was trying to sabotage me.

This was another of the best days of my life. Like a scene from a movie. A SWAT team swooped in and, in approximately fifteen minutes, hauled away the company computers. I arranged for this to happen on a Wednesday when I knew that James and many of the others would not be in the office, but it was tricky because my service department manager came in at 6:30 a.m., and I had to keep him in the dark.

James eventually found out what I was doing. He hurried back to the office, but by this point, the team was almost done. And I had had them secure James's hard drive first, and then the finance director's, so by the time he got there, we were almost done.

I was at my Hyundai dealership, and James came in and thundered, "Get down here! I need to talk to you!"

I said to my lawyer, "Clara, you have to come with me. I don't know what he's capable of." I knew he had a violent personality. He had put some of my managers in a chokehold. "Should we call the police?" I asked. "Have backup?"

Clara was a big woman. "Relax. We got this," she said.

When we got to James's office, James said, "What are you doing? You have no right. Have I not been good to you? I've never lied to you." He pointed to his Rolex watch and said, "I swear to you. You can take this watch off me right now if I'm lying to you. I don't know why you keep thinking that I stole from you and that I'm doing the wrong thing by you."

"Yeah, whatever," I said, walking away.

James's computer told a different story. In his hard drive

was an email he had sent to his wife that read something like, *I'm going to destroy her. She's going to be penniless. Don't worry. I'll have these three dealerships all to myself in a few months. We got this.* That was when I learned that James's wife was also in cahoots with him.

Did I find anything on the hard drives that I could use against James in court? Clara thought so. Proof that my employees knew that I was paying the other dealership's bills—and that the vendors knew as well. And evidence that James was trying to take over and had some key managers helping him.

But I didn't pursue it. Not with Clara. Because for all that she was doing to help me, I had a sinking suspicion that she was robbing me blind too.

* * *

Although it felt like everyone was out to get me during this time, I did have some help. A couple who had worked for Pride a few years prior—one was a sales manager, the other worked in the finance department—saw what was happening. They contacted me and basically said, "Look, we don't think the right thing's going on there. We know James is a crook, and half your staff is probably stealing from you. Maybe we can at least guide you and help you look at your financials."

I would meet them at least once a week and go over things. They helped me learn the industry lingo and clean house, and they were instrumental in my hiring a whole new advertising firm.

And they also helped me with the used car auctions.

"You need to start going to the auctions," they told me.

A used car auction is where we send cars on our lot that

are not selling in order to recoup some profit. How it works is we send the auction a "run list" of the cars we want to auction, and they come to get the cars and prep them to sell.

The auctions were on Wednesdays, and James usually went (which was why I knew he wouldn't be around when Clara and I sent in the SWAT team to take all the computer hard drives). The auction allots your dealership a certain time frame, and you get to stand on a box and sell your cars. Not much different from how auctions are portrayed in the movies.

Although he went every Wednesday, James never told me he was going. He would just say something like, "Oh, I'm going to my parents' gravesite. I'm religious, and I want to tell them how much I love them." Then he would bring lunch for the whole office afterward, so of course, all the employees thought he was great.

Why did James want to go to the auction? So he could make some money under the table. As an example, let's say, according to Pride's bookkeeping, James showed a car at auction that he sold for $1,000. But off book, James would bring down the price to $700 and then pocket the $300. The dealership only made $700, not $1,000. Or he might sell the car at a higher price, if there was a lot of interest, and only put $1,000 on the books and pocket the rest. He had a nice scam going.

Every Wednesday, when James got back from the auction, I would see that I made $1,000 on a car and never realize I only had $700 to show for it. And because I wasn't privy to the books, I couldn't figure out why I was losing money at the auctions. Even when I took over the bookkeeping, the checks I received from the new car sales made it seem like we were making money, so I didn't realize that our finances had sprung a giant leak. If James went to four auctions a month with ten to twenty cars each time and pocketed hundreds of dollars with each sale, I was losing thousands and thousands of dollars each month.

"You need to rep your own cars," my friends told me.

One day, I said to James, "Why don't I take over the used car auctions?"

"You don't need to do that," he said.

"No, I really want to start going. I want to learn."

He continued to try to dissuade me. "No, you really don't want to go. It's too cold. As a woman, you won't like it."

I pushed and pushed. I wouldn't take no for an answer. Finally, he relented. I wrote down the day I started going to the auction in a book that I kept during this time: *March 16, 2016*. And I also wrote, *James getting annoyed with me*. Of course he was annoyed! I was getting in the way of his scamming.

When I started going to the auction, I sold all my cars for the prices that were on the books, and, lo and behold, I started making my money back.

At this point, I was taking everything over. Even though I didn't know what I was talking about, I just started doing things—calling vendors, making demands, taking over parts of the business, firing, hiring. James started coming into the office less and less until finally he didn't come to work for a whole nine months.

But what did he care? I was paying him, and he was running his other dealership.

I finally asked my lawyer, Clara, "Why am I paying him? Can't I at least take some of his pay away?"

She said no. By law, I had to pay him. He was still a Pride employee. He still had 10 percent ownership of Hyundai and Kia, 20 percent ownership of Chevy, and 40 percent ownership of Chrysler-Dodge-Jeep, which wasn't even our dealership because neither Michael nor I ever signed any paperwork!

He was living the high life while I felt like I was drowning.

But all that was about to come to a crashing halt. I knew it. James knew it. He knew the end was near. By March 2016, James couldn't take it anymore, and during those nine months when he didn't come into the office, Clara went back and forth with James's lawyer trying to figure out a way to get him out of there for good. (And I was paying for all that legal time. *Cha-ching!*)

Finally, James agreed to let me buy him out of Pride in the summer of 2016. And once he got his payout, I never heard from him again.

I felt like I could walk into my own business and finally breathe. But I was also scared to be in charge of a company I had no idea how to run.

By this time, I had gotten rid of a lot of the people who had been messing with me. Not everyone. I was still swimming with a lot of sharks. Just not the major sharks. They were gone.

As all this was happening, I would go home and have such anxiety all night long. *I'm going to fail. I'm not going to be able to do this.* I really didn't have anyone I could talk to. My sister? My friends? I didn't feel like they would understand. Plus, I was embarrassed. How could I have let all this happen? Why didn't I pay attention to what was happening at Pride while Michael was alive?

"Well, why don't you just sell it?" a friend of mine asked. She didn't know I still had three huge mortgages on the dealerships because my partner stole millions of dollars from me.

I had people in the business say to me, "Well, that was dumb. Why would you want to take over a car dealership when you have no knowledge about the car business?" But I didn't think it was dumb because at the time my kids were driving me. I knew how much my son wanted the business. I knew how hard my in-laws worked until the day they died. I wanted my kids, and my in-laws, to know that I did everything possible to keep the business afloat. I wanted to make them proud of me.

In the end, after all James's shenanigans, all he got was a slap on the wrist—and money from me. I could not believe that I had to pay *him*. Clara did not do right by me when it came to James. She didn't do anything to prove that he stole and forged and mismanaged. She kept saying, "Well, at least I got you to buy him out," and I thought, *You did nothing*. What's worse is I thought of her as a friend and saw her often for meals, not realizing that, like William, she was billing me for all of it. I would pay her for work that was never finished, and she would say, "Hey, but at least we tried." Like William, she wasn't an automotive lawyer, so she could bluff and talk a good game, and in the end it was about our *quantity* of time rather than the quality. I ended up spending a million dollars on Clara's services, in addition to the million dollars I paid to James to leave the business.

I finally let Clara go. I don't think she believed me at first when I told her that I no longer needed her services. She thought I would be toast without her, but I felt like I was toast *with* her because I kept getting burned!

At the time, I didn't realize how much money all this really was. And while I was spending money on lawyers and everything else, my dealerships were taking a huge hit. My expenses at Chevy, in particular, were $400,000 a month, and I was only taking in $300,000 a month, so I was moving $100,000 every month to that one dealership.

It wasn't until after James left that I found out how much he was hurting my business from within, particularly my Kia and Hyundai stores. James put all the money into Chevy, where he had the bigger stake, so he could pay his employees and vendors at his own dealership. And all the employees I fired? Most of them went to work for James.

And took my customers with them.

That was how I started *really* losing money.

And that was when my car manufacturers had had enough. I was in danger of losing it all.

Chapter 11

SUZANNE, DEALMAKER

BY 2016, THE DEALERSHIPS WERE LOSING MILLIONS OF dollars annually—a fact that I was unaware of. Part of the problem was I had little knowledge of the business and had put my trust into the people who were running it, but I was hoping to change all that.

Liam was my parts and service director for all three dealerships. With James gone, he had decided that he was going to take me under his wing and help me get into the good graces of the employees. Frankly, I should have known better. But I was desperate. And for some crazy reason, he thought the best way to do this was to give the employees a raise. Give more money away from a business that was hemorrhaging? Exactly. Not a good idea. But I was willing to try anything.

"You know, before James was here and it was just Michael," Liam said, "the employees had more paid holidays."

I started giving the employees paid holidays. I did whatever Liam said because I thought it was the right thing to do. He had been with my husband for eight years, and I believed he would do right by me, even though there were obvious issues—obvious only because I was beginning to figure out how to actually *run* a car dealership.

As the fixed operational manager for all three dealerships, Liam should have been improving my numbers in parts and service, but he wasn't. They were not generating enough income. And there were some glaring discrepancies. The math wasn't adding up. For example, instead of having one locksmith for all three dealerships, we had one for each, and each locksmith had a different fee. Why were things being done this way? Because each manager who hired a locksmith got a kickback. *Cha-ching!*

* * *

So my remaining employees were getting kickbacks, paid holidays, and higher-than-average salaries. No wonder none of them wanted to leave. They knew even if they managed to get hired somewhere else, they'd never make what Pride was paying them.

When I brought that up, Liam apologized.

"Look, I did things that I'm not proud of," he told me, "but James was a bully, and I couldn't afford to lose my job."

Part of me understood that, but James was gone now, and Liam was still not doing the right thing. I may have gotten rid of the host virus, but everything around it had been contaminated.

Expenses were even more out of control because I gave my employees everything they wanted—in particular, expensive equipment for the dealerships that we didn't need. (And my vendor-partners said they would help with revenue but didn't.) Even though I couldn't afford it at the time, I paid for anything that made their lives easier at Pride, but none of it generated any revenue or brought any growth into my dealerships. In so many ways, James was still controlling the puppet strings, even though he was no longer with the company.

I decided to take a different approach. I contacted my manufacturers: Hyundai, Kia, and Chevy. By now, they were doing business with both Pride and James's newly renamed dealership. I said to my vendors, "How dare you! How did you allow this to happen? If I stay with you, it's either going to be him or me. You can't do business with us both. I need to know where your loyalty is."

It was an uphill battle. (Everything was.) Of course, as James was easing his way out of Pride, he told my vendors I had no idea what I was doing. He was right, of course. I didn't, but I was trying to learn. "I don't know why she wants to be there," he told them. "It'll be a disaster."

But the truth was I hadn't done anything differently than Michael had, other than hiring a new advertising firm and changing the company's logo. I didn't know enough to change anything. The reason the businesses were failing was James's mismanagement—and the fact that he had been stealing from me for months, probably years, and then making it look like I was the one who was incompetent.

But now James was finally out. And I knew this was my chance. And as hard as it was, I was going to make the most of it.

In mid-2016, a team of Hyundai executives from corporate called a meeting in Burlington, Massachusetts, to go over sales and service with surrounding dealers. One of Hyundai's head district managers called to tell me that he and the Eastern regional director wanted to discuss some terms about running my Hyundai dealership. Later that month, the head district manager visited my dealership to walk around and observe how my sales and service departments were being handled.

He was not happy.

He made it clear that Hyundai was not about to hand over its dealership to me. As far as Hyundai was concerned, I wasn't a dealer principal. I had no legal connection to the business. I was inexperienced. But what I did have was a connection to the Pride legacy: I had been married to a principal who was a second-generation dealership owner. And I had a passion, an intense desire, to make it work. That was it.

To their credit, Hyundai executives decided to give me a chance, but they had three conditions for me:

1. Go to Korea to better understand the product, watch how cars were made, and learn about Korean culture.
2. Join a "20 Group," a peer/consultant group that offered expertise and resources and met on a quarterly basis to go over every aspect of the dealership in a financial composite, a numbers document that outlined expense and profit.
3. Go to the NADA Academy and take a series of classes that combined instruction with hands-on practical applications.

I was petrified at the prospect of all this but also so naive about the whole situation. If I knew then how tough it would be to accomplish these requirements, I probably would not have gone through with it. But sometimes in life, you're better off not knowing how cold the water is till you get in.

* * *

In 2016 and 2018, as part of my promise to Hyundai, I took two trips to Seoul. Financially speaking, I probably had no right going on these trips. Each one cost approximately $10,000, and my dealership didn't have the money. In addition to all the nonsense I was going through with James and his wrecking crew, a former comptroller had also been stealing from me and had done damage to my bottom line, but I was committed to Hyundai and wanted to maintain a good business relationship, so I decided to weather the expense.

Mikey came with me for the first trip, which was for all new Hyundai dealers and included a tour of the Hyundai Steel plant in Dangjin, Korea's first privately funded integrated steelworks.

I asked my then-new comptroller, Daisy, to come with me to Seoul in 2018. Rather than a series of facility tours, this second trip to Seoul was for Hyundai's annual meeting. Daisy had worked for my in-laws and my husband back in the day and was available when I had to fire my comptroller. Although I had been hesitant to hire Daisy because my in-laws had fired her, she was familiar with the business and, let's face it, I was desperate. I felt like I didn't have a choice.

Things didn't start off smoothly. When she arrived, I found out she didn't know the computer system, and then she began hiring all her friends and moving money around to the departments where the people she knew made money so they could get more of a bonus. Although my expenses were through the roof, she kept telling me they were in line with dealership standards. I would sit down with Daisy and my accountant and question why we weren't making money, and she would be full of excuses and false promises. I ended up letting Daisy go after a year.

With my first trip to Korea completed, I needed to check

off another item on my Hyundai list: joining a 20 Group. A 20 Group consists of twenty Hyundai dealers from around the United States that meet quarterly to share best practices and network. They go over a composite, a financial document that details everything aspect of their business—from how many office people are staffed at a dealership to what their salaries should be. By going over the composite quarterly, dealers can better assess whether they are making or losing money.

Just what I needed.

I started attending 20 Group meetings in July 2016 and didn't know what to expect. My general manager at the time, Doug, said, "Oh, don't worry. I'll go with you and be your spokesperson. I'll get you through this so you can be appointed dealer principal."

I was skeptical. And uncomfortable. Doug was inappropriate with me at the office sometimes. He would tell me that he had dreams about me that he would never want his wife to know. He would make advances, like when he was using the copy machine, his printouts would "somehow" fall on the floor, and he would say things like, "Hey, can you bend over a little more?" It was like a scene straight out of *9 to 5*. He always stood a little too close when he was explaining or teaching something. At first, he made these advances in his office when we were alone, but over time he began doing it around other managers. Even vendors from outside companies noticed.

But at the time, I felt handcuffed. I don't know how else to explain it. I didn't have anybody who could take his role. Yes, he was a pervert, but he knew a lot. What I didn't know at the time was that he was hiding a lot too.

The first 20 Group meeting was in Maine. I live in the northeast, but this was way up there in Bar Harbor, which was a five-hour drive. Doug told me to stop by his house to pick him up so we could drive up together. I didn't love the idea of being cooped up in the car with him, but I knew that if he crossed the line, no matter how desperate I was, I would terminate him.

As we were on the road, he told me, "When we get there, I'll do all the talking. Don't worry."

"I'm not worried," I said, "but that's why I'm going, right? To learn." "No, it's better to let me do the talking."

At first, there were only ten dealers in our 20 Group, so they were happy at the prospect of having me join. How it works is after an initial meeting, the members of the group decide if they like what a prospective dealer principal has to offer. If they do, they invite the principal to join.

Turns out, I had almost the same composite in terms of size and staff as another dealer in upstate New York that was doing very well. I thought, *Wow, I want to be like this guy*. At the initial meeting, Doug wouldn't let me have any input. My feeling was the only way I was going to learn was by asking questions. He disagreed and thought it better that I didn't "embarrass" myself. I felt like a wife whose husband was saying, "Oh, shut up, honey. You don't know what you're talking about. I'll do everything." It felt like Michael all over again.

Meanwhile, the members of my prospective 20 Group sensed something was wrong with the dynamic between Doug and me. I didn't know them, and they didn't know me, but I could tell they were annoyed, like, *Who the hell is this GM, and why is she letting him work for her? He's totally taking advantage of her.* Doug dismissed any input I gave, and they could sense that he wanted more from me than just the boss-employee relationship.

I made it through the three days and was thrilled when I was invited to join. When I went to the next meeting in Key West three months later, I had already fired Doug. When I walked in, the guys asked, "Oh, where's Doug?" and I told them that I had to let him go.

"Thank god," they said. Although they were still getting to know me, they could already see that Doug was bad news, and they were happy to see that I had discovered that too.

The 20 Group meetings are three-day affairs. We have a general topic that we want to discuss, and we do homework so that when we get there, we are prepared and can hit the ground running. The composite sheet allows us to narrow down every single thing that we're doing, whether it's with our service departments, sales departments, or advisory staffs. We try to work on one aspect of the business because even in three days we can't cover it all. Topics can be as minor as, *Oh, my god, I didn't realize that if I talked to this vendor, I could save myself a thousand dollars a year*! Or it might be a new initiative that will bring another $100,000 to the bottom line. Each time, it's different, and every time I go, it's empowering, and I learn something new. We also have contests to see who has come up with the best idea for their business in the months leading up to the meeting, something that's either making money or better positioning the dealership—an idea that other dealers might want to implement. We have a kitty of about $100, and whoever has the best idea wins it. I even won the kitty once (although at this moment, I can't remember what my idea was).

Early on, that upstate New York dealer that I hoped to emulate sent his GM to the meeting, and I learned a lot from him, but that dealer eventually left our group for another one.

There were two Hyundai 20 Groups in my region when

I joined. In the first, most of the dealers were doing well and making a lot of money. That was the one the upstate New York GM wanted to join. My group, unfortunately, was mostly losing money. One kid took the business over from his dad, so he was learning the ropes like me, although he had more experience than I did. Another dealership was losing a lot of money, and the principal had just taken it over and was trying to build it up. Everyone seemed to have a different woe story, but we were all in the same boat—some dealerships were just losing more money than others.

I was bleeding the most—gifting employees everything they wanted, buying unnecessary equipment and supplies, and, essentially, trying to please everybody so I wouldn't have a mass exodus. But I slowly got more comfortable and educated, and by the sixth or seventh meeting of my 20 Group, I was asking the right questions and engaging. I was becoming in tune with how I could better my business, whether it was my service drive or sales floor. I went from *I don't know anything* to *I don't want to embarrass myself* to *I don't care. I need to learn this, and I need to put my big girl pants on* to *I think I'm getting the hang of this.*

I was starting, for the first time in a long time, to feel good—more confident—about myself. Especially as a woman in a predominantly male business. Women running car dealerships are rare. I am the only female dealer principal in my 20 Group. Most of the women I have met or read about are either siblings of the dealer or daughters who have taken over the business, or even a wife who had some type of role in the dealership before her husband passed away. But most of the women who took over the business after their husband died had a supportive staff that guided them along until they had a handle on things. I can't think of anyone else who took over a business with a partner who was determined to see her fail, who lost millions of dollars, and who was on a deserted island, alone, with more than a hundred vultures feasting on her.

I had done what I thought I could never do. And I had met two of Hyundai's objectives so far. I'd gone to Korea, and I'd joined a 20 Group. All that was left was the NADA Academy. It was time to go back to school.

Chapter 12

SUZANNE, STUDENT

THE NATIONAL AUTOMOBILE DEALERS ASSOCIATION (NADA) Academy consists of six one-week classroom sessions held over the course of a year at NADA headquarters in Tysons, Virginia. The sessions are combined with hands-on practical application in each area of the dealership, such as accounting principles, inventory investment, and service departments.

I was happy to go. I wanted to learn as much as I could and prove that I could take this on—to Hyundai and to myself. But the idea of sitting alongside veteran dealership executives and principals was daunting. Like flying to Korea, I really didn't want to do it alone. At the time, I still didn't have a handle on any part of my dealership, so I wanted someone to go with me, someone I knew, someone who would be part of my "team."

I asked Liam, my parts and service director for the three dealerships. He had always wanted to go—a NADA Academy graduation certificate is good to have on your résumé. I thought that while we attended, he could teach me what we were missing in the aspects of the dealership that he oversaw.

We began taking classes in November 2016. We flew to Tysons, Virginia, and spent a week there, and then went five more times in the next year. Liam offered to take care of all the arrangements each time. He booked us on JetBlue and at the Ritz-Carlton, which was the hotel nearby where most of the students stayed. I appreciated that he was making the effort. What I didn't realize until later was that Liam had ulterior motives. The expenses for these trips, which totaled about $10,000 per person, not including airfare, hotel, or meals, were covered by the dealership, and Liam charged them to the company's credit cards. No problem there. But he had been redeeming the points and frequent flyer miles that were accruing with every purchase and using them for personal perks—trips with his wife, etc.

And that was just the tip of the iceberg. Liam wasn't all that interested in being a team player, and despite his many years of employment with Pride, *he* had a lot to learn.

Before we left for Virginia that first time, Hyundai required us to take a test with fifty or sixty questions to gauge our knowledge of every part of the dealership, from office and sales to service and parts. Because I knew virtually nothing, I asked my GM, my office manager, and Liam to help me answer the questions. I figured that with those three at my side, we had sixty years of experience in the room.

We scored a 50 percent.

That was concerning. These were the people running the dealerships, and they didn't know the answers? I thought, *My god, how bad is this?*

When I finally arrived at school, I knew immediately I was in over my head. The class was made up of thirty-two men and six women, and as we introduced ourselves, I quickly found that everyone else had been in the automotive business forever, even the younger students who were dealer principal children. Very intimidating. On top of that, virtually every student scored in the nineties on every test we took while I floundered. Even the teachers seemed to look at me and think, *What is she doing here?* I felt like I was back in the third grade. I wasn't good enough. That first week I hardly participated because I was afraid of making a fool of myself.

And it got worse. Then came the dreadful "composite," which analyzed individual and group stats on profitability, expense absorption, and employee productivity across each department of the dealership, from parts to payroll to service. My dealerships were at the bottom of the barrel. My expenses were triple everyone else's, and I wasn't bringing in enough gross to cover my expenses. Things didn't look good.

My service department, in particular, was not making any money—in fact, we were losing money every month. When I asked Liam about it, since he was in charge of service and parts, he gave me every excuse in the book. He blamed the techs or said we didn't have the right parts. I learned later that was all nonsense. He let his employees get away with murder because he didn't like confrontation and wanted everyone to like him. Of course, I didn't know that then. And because I had no history in the business, I had no choice but to believe what he said.

As was my longstanding habit, I became riddled with anxiety—about the enormity of the information I needed to know, the dire situation of my business, and what I was learning about the people who worked for me. James may have been gone, but things still seemed to be getting worse. The first night, I called my kids.

"Look," I said. "I failed the test. I'm the oldest in the class." Another guy was older than I was, but he had been in the business for twenty years and knew what he was doing. "I don't know anything. I'm a fish out of water. I don't think I can do this."

"No, Mom," they said. "You have to. You're strong."

They believed in me, so I stuck with it. As that first week and the subsequent weeks went on, I realized that I wasn't going to be able to rely on Liam. I needed to start relying on myself.

Some other students and I formed a little study group. There was an area downstairs from the classrooms where you could buy lunch. Our study group met there to go over the information each day and test one another. I asked Liam if he would like to join.

"Oh, no, I don't need to go," he told me. "I'm okay. I'm going to go back to the hotel and take a nap." He never attended.

When we had homework, I'd try to encourage him. "Come on. Let's do it together."

He would say, "We have so much time," and then wait for the last minute, or his work would be half-assed. At the end of that first week at NADA, we retook the test we had taken at the beginning as a final exam. I got a 90 percent. Liam got a 69.

I was proud of myself for doing so well and furious that he scored so low. NADA Academy was costing my company $40,000 for Liam and me to attend (an amount that—I didn't realize at the time—I didn't have). Plus, I paid for every meal, whether we ate in the cafeteria or walked next door to Smith & Wollensky or one of the nice restaurants at the mall. Nothing was cheap. And he was taking naps? And nodding off in class? And skipping homework assignments? School was teaching me as much about Liam as it was about the automotive dealership business. That first trip was an eye-opener.

Each time I returned to Tysons, I tried to learn as much as I could. We learned about parts one week, and I brought my parts manager along so that he could learn how to improve and what we were missing to make more of a profit.

By late 2016 and early 2017, I was losing $200,000 *a month* in my dealerships. Times that by twelve months in a year, and I was going underwater quickly. But I decided to take things one step at a time. I was just trying to get through it.

As the sessions continued and my knowledge increased, my eyes began to open more and more. I learned about what it takes to run a successful car dealership and also about what was going on under my nose at home. Everything was about simple math: If you have eight technicians and twelve areas to fix cars, then you need four more technicians to be at your full potential. Additionally, you need those technicians to be busy at all times during the day to make a profit, so if they have three jobs a day that only require an hour each, then they are free for five more hours if they are working an eight-hour day.

With that simple knowledge, it was easy to see that my service departments weren't up to their capacity. There was supposed to be chaos at all times, and my departments were like a morgue. Meanwhile, we were losing customers to other dealerships. Retention is everything if you want to be successful.

I also realized that Liam—the team player I had been hoping to count on, the one who was supposed to show me the ropes—had his own agenda, a mindset that was polluting the business, especially the employees who reported to him.

Before we went to school together, I thought Liam was doing right by me. When he said, "We need to give our employees paid holidays," or "We need to hire these people," I believed him, never realizing he was just doing whatever was best for himself financially and for the guys who reported to him. He didn't say, "Hey, we're not meeting our goals. This is what we have to do to change things around." He just let people do whatever they wanted and let the business hemorrhage.

Yet throughout 2016 and 2017, I was getting stronger. Things were slowly starting to make sense. I was understanding key aspects and paying attention to things I hadn't been looking at before, including the financial statements at the end of each month, which gave me all the numbers of the dealership, including our profit and loss.

A lot of people in the class that first week felt bad for me, probably thinking, *This girl is going to drown*. I bet everyone in the class would be shocked to know that I am still in business and to see how far I've come. The teachers saw firsthand what I did not know and what I struggled with and tried to help me.

In October 2017, I graduated from the NADA Academy. My kids, who were both in college at the time, flew down for the graduation, and so did a friend. It was a really nice day. I was so excited and proud of myself. There was a photo of my graduation class in *Automotive News*. Liam bought me a Montblanc pen for graduation as a congratulatory gift. The old Suzanne would have thought, *How sweet*. But the new Suzanne knew better. New Suzanne thought, *How much did this cost me?* I knew he charged it to Pride.

During my time at the NADA Academy, I had gained more than just automotive knowledge. I gained a lot of insight. I felt empowered. I knew what I had to do when I got home. First on the list: I had to let Liam go.

I knew that would be difficult because he allowed people to do what they wanted. I knew things would get worse before they got better, but how could I keep somebody I didn't trust?

About a week after we came back, I said to Liam, "You know, after going to school with you and seeing some other aspects of you, I am really disappointed that I allowed myself to believe in you and trust in you." Things had to change. At the very least, Liam's department was doing a shitty job. I was paying him all this money to learn and grow, and he wasn't interested in making any changes to better himself or my bottom line. It was discouraging, and I just had to keep myself upbeat or else I feared I would sink into a depression, and I couldn't let that happen.

I had kids to raise. And a business to run.

If I hadn't gone to the Academy, I probably would have been bankrupt and out of business in a year or two. I owe a lot to Hyundai for making me go and for convincing me to join the 20 Group. You don't know what you don't know, and I didn't know anything.

* * *

Once Hyundai was under control, the executives at Kia were willing to negotiate with me, but they began losing patience. I would have been a Kia dealer faster, but Clara had been jacking around their lawyer and the regional director—so much so that I almost didn't become a Kia dealer at all! Clara would say things like, "Don't back off. You've got to be strong. We have to stick to our guns," and I believed her. But I should have said, "This is what they want. Let's give it to them. It's not unreasonable. Let's call it a day." Instead of costing me $10,000 for legal services, it cost me $50,000. Finally, by January 2017, I urged Clara to agree to Kia's terms, and everything was resolved. That left just one more dealership to convince: General Motors.

Of all three dealerships, getting Chevrolet to sign on with me was the hardest. Mostly because when I took over, my general manager, Doug, had whispered in Chevy's ear, "Suzanne doesn't know what she's doing. She doesn't want to know. She's going to run this place into the ground." Badmouthing me. Like James.

For years, Doug had been on the General Motors dealership council, where he was supposed to represent us and fight for us. Instead, he fed my GM rep all sorts of nonsense. To make matters worse, once James left, I made Doug the general manager for all three dealerships without knowing he was badmouthing me.

The General Motors people gave me a really tough time. I scheduled a meeting with a rep, and one day I was in my husband's office at the Chevy dealership, and I could see my employees all whispering. A short man in a well-tailored suit had walked in. He looked angry. I knew immediately he was the Chevy rep. And I was already intimidated.

"I need to talk with you," he said once he got into my office. "Your sales are dropping because James is gone."

They were blaming *me* for the drop in sales?

"Why kick James out when he was giving us so much business?" he asked. "You have no business being here. We can easily take this away from you."

It was Hyundai and Kia all over again, but worse. I felt threatened. Bullied. I remember being so nervous when he left, thinking, *This guy is a total dick.*

But soon, with James gone, the Chevy numbers started

improving. Chevy eased the reins. And when that started happening, Doug started changing his tune with Chevy. "Oh, she *does* want to learn!"

Not long after, that creepy Chevy rep got promoted, and I never had to see him again. They replaced him with a woman named Cameron who didn't seem like she wanted to be at that job for long. She wanted a higher position, so she was thrilled to get me under her wing and say, "Okay, what do we have to do to get this done?" I was thrilled too. Cameron helped me tremendously. A lot of times a rep will come in and just say, "You need to work on this," but Cameron got into the weeds with me. She pointed out weaknesses and told me what I needed to concentrate on. She made game plans and helped turn things around. She sent someone into the dealership to review stats every month for *years* until I became dealer principal in September 2019. She gave me everything I needed to get me started and make this work, and I'm indebted to her. She's no longer my rep after she got some bigwig job at GM that she totally deserved. And while I miss that teamwork, I'm more than happy for her.

The car business is like an octopus with multiple legs that you need to pay attention to. At the NADA Academy, I learned that if I concentrated on every department at the same time, I would get overwhelmed and accomplish nothing. I needed to triage. If I tried fixing one thing at a time, I might gain some headway. Especially now that I had people working with me rather than against me. The cheaters. The liars. The thieves. They were all gone. I had dug myself out of a ditch. Now it was time to start climbing a mountain.

Chapter 13

SUZANNE, GIRLFRIEND 2.0

IT PROBABLY COMES AS NO SURPRISE THAT WHILE everything was going on with Pride in 2016, I started seeing a therapist on occasion. I needed *someone* to talk to. Between James, Doug, and my lawyers looking to milk me dry, and with my kids still reeling from their father's death, I needed to let off some steam. I told her all the crazy stuff I had going on in my life, and she calmly said things like, "Well, maybe you should go for a massage."

A massage? Really? Sure, that'll fix, maybe, one afternoon.

I didn't even have time to get my nails done back then, let alone get my back done. The only luxury I allowed myself was twice a week I got my hair blown out because I don't like doing my hair. I did try my therapist's suggestion and went for a few massages because I was carrying so much stress in my back and I got to a point where I couldn't sit down, but other than that, the therapist just wasn't getting to the root of my problems or helping my anxiety.

And then I met someone.

Through Clara of all people.

While Clara and I were working together, we began to develop a friendship—or so I thought. During this time, Clara had been talking about a guy who would be "perfect" for me, and her wife, Diane, also brought this person up to me.

"Have you started dating?" Diane asked me.

"Dating? No. First, I don't have time. Second, I have no interest." I hadn't looked at a guy in twenty-something years.

"I know, but you have so much on your plate, and it would be nice for you to just have someone to talk to," Diane said. "I know this guy, Steve, who you might like. You should meet him. You, Steve, Clara, and I should go out together, someplace casual."

I kept saying no, no, no, and then Clara and Diane found out in February 2016 that some of my close friends, three couples, were planning to throw me a really nice steak-house dinner party for my fiftieth birthday. Diane said, "I can bring Steve by on your birthday. We'll be sitting at the bar, and we can just kind of come over and say hi. If you wanna go out with him, great. If you don't, you don't have to. No pressure."

I admit the idea appealed to me. Most of my girlfriends at the time were married, so everyone was going to be coupled at my birthday dinner except for me. On Friday and Saturday nights, I basically just sat at home. I think that's part of the reason I worked so much—because I really had nothing else to do.

The night of my dinner, I casually looked over toward the bar and saw the three of them. My first thought was *Oh, he's a nice-looking guy*. He had gray hair and seemed fit. I told the couples at the table what was going on, and they urged me to go over and say hi.

I was a nervous wreck. I hadn't been introduced to a guy

in more than twenty years. But I summoned up some courage and walked over.

"Hi. I'm Suzanne." I shook his hand. "Nice to meet you." I could tell he was interested.

The problem was I wasn't. Not really. I had no desire to get married again—or even date again. My marriage had scarred me, and I wasn't yearning to revisit that kind of life. I thought, *I don't think I can do this.*

They ended up coming over to our table when the restaurant waitstaff brought out the cake, and Steve and I talked for a bit about his work in Asia. He was an engineer of some kind. And then we exchanged phone numbers, and he left.

I thought, *Whew, that's over with!* When I'm nervous, I talk a mile a minute, and I probably didn't give Steve time to get a word in. But truthfully, it wasn't as bad as I thought it would be. He was very quiet. Polite. The kind of guy who held the door for you. A real gentleman. But he wasn't much of a talker. That put more pressure on me to carry the conversation. And I felt like I was carrying enough at the time.

He texted me the next day:

I have a business trip coming up. I'll be gone for a week, but when I get back, I would love to take you out.

I started calling my friends. "What do I do? I don't know what to do."

"Stick to your guns," one friend said. "He's interested. It doesn't matter that you're leading the whole conversation and he's not getting a word in."

So I said that I would go out with him. And we ended up dating for three years.

Our relationship was hard to describe. We didn't want to live with each other, and we didn't want to get married. Maybe it was because of where we were in our lives. Steve had been married for fifteen years and had three kids, and one day his wife came to him and announced she wanted a divorce. Then he was in another relationship for nine years, and that didn't end well either. We both had trust issues.

It was kind of like a friend thing—it was nice to have someplace to go on a Saturday night. I wasn't sitting at home anymore. But I knew right away it wasn't going to be long term. I didn't have time for a full-blown relationship.

I think I initially liked Steve because he was so different from Michael. He was tall; Michael was short. They didn't have one thing in common. But I wasn't in love with him. I was in love with the fact that he was not Michael. We didn't yell at each other. There was no emotion, which, of course, does not make for a healthy relationship, but at the time I thought, *This is great!*

I went out with him longer than I probably should have, but he became a de facto therapist. I didn't hear from him much during the week—he would text me once a night to say, *Hey. Hope you had a great day. Good night.* But he never called me. We maybe talked on the phone twice in three years—and one time was when I almost died at the car auction (a horrific accident happened two seconds after I was standing right there—I was very lucky).

Sometimes we went away on weekends. We both liked tennis, and he ran triathlons, but I needed a relationship where both parties were represented equally. Something I didn't have with Michael, and I knew I needed. My therapist had been telling me for six months, "He's not for you," but it was hard to let Steve go. To me, he was like a warm blanket. And I needed that at the time.

I didn't tell my kids about Steve. It was only about two and a half years after my husband died, so I still felt like I was cheating on Michael. I only told a few of my friends and my sister. I was mortified if I saw people out in public and just said, "This is Steve." I didn't say we were dating, and if anyone asked me about him later, I'd say, "Oh, he's a vendor for the dealership" or something like that.

But the more we were together, the more I saw other sides of him. Sides that were more like Michael. He got angry. He could be very opinionated. He liked things done his way. He wasn't a big eater but liked to drink. And he could be snobby, making fun of the way people dressed or the cars they drove (he had a Mercedes).

When we went to the movies, he got into arguments with people. Somehow, we always managed to sit behind a person with a cell phone that went off or two people who talked in the middle of the movie. Steve seemed mild-mannered, but I can't tell you how many times I thought he was going to get into a fist fight with someone, which reminded me of Michael. And of my father.

I finally broke it off. I would probably still be dating him today if it were up to him. He was happy with a nonchalant relationship, but I wasn't. I was put off by his snobbery, drinking, and controlling behavior. I wasn't the same Suzanne who married a guy because he bought her things or stayed with him after he cheated on her. I wanted more. I didn't want to settle anymore.

Chapter 14

SUZANNE, PRESIDENT, PRIDE MOTOR GROUP

BY EARLY 2020, THINGS WERE STARTING TO MAKE SENSE at Pride. I knew more than a little about everything, which was enough to keep the business going. I finally hired people I could handle. And trust. And we started to make a little bit of money.

And then COVID-19 hit.

One step forward, two steps back.

I used to sell a hundred cars a month in one store. After COVID-19, that number went down to fifty. Sometimes even fewer than that, which meant we had no choice but to raise our prices. For the first time in automobile history, people paid sticker price or over because they needed a car, so while we were selling fewer cars, we were making more per car. That was the compromise. Most customers understood and knew we weren't hiding anything, but it was still a tough sell in an economy that had tanked. I knew some dealers took advantage of this situation, but I vowed that I was going to run my business honestly and with integrity, and I hoped customers would keep coming back. So far, they have.

My biggest problem became my service departments. Virtually nobody was driving anywhere in 2020. Then, over the next few years, as people ventured outdoors again, demand increased, but it became hard to find technicians and service people. Normally, a dealership makes its money on the "back end," or service department, but COVID-19 forced us to rely on the "front end," or sales, and that was difficult. But as the months and years moved on, we continued to learn from our mistakes and work hard.

Six years after the death of my husband, the year 2020 marked the first that my company made money.

I'm really proud of that.

My goal had been to be in the black by the end of that year. I wound up making $1.2 million in profit. Out of the original 20 Group dealers I met in Maine, I made the most money that year.

It was an incredible turnaround, considering every month I had been sweating it out. *How much am I going to lose? What department will lose the most?* Fast forward, and now I'm asking myself, *How much money am I going to make?* I know I'm going to make money every month. It might not be $100,000. It might be $20,000, but at least I know I'm in the black. It took six years, and I had to do it on my own, but I did it.

I can honestly say that I feel good about where I am right now. It wasn't easy, but that's okay. Things in life don't come easy, right? My childhood taught me that. Throughout this whole process, not only has the business been through a grueling time, but so have I.

Still, I try to focus on the good. Being surrounded by all

that bad taught me that. Yes, my father was manic-depressive, but the truth is that I've never been a person who couldn't get out of bed or who thought she just couldn't go on. If I ever have a bad day, I always give myself a pep talk, probably because I've never had anyone else to do that for me. I think regularly, *You know what, Suzanne? You're not on the streets with your two kids, worrying about how you're going to feed them.* I try to remind myself that I'm very lucky. Just being able to write in this book that I have lost millions of dollars and come out on the other side in the black is a blessing.

Each year, I get stronger and more confident, and I focus on making sure that my kids are okay. When the anniversary of Michael's death rolls around, I also make sure that they are busy. For my son, Mikey, who is now the manager of my used car department, it's still really difficult.

On Christmas Eve 2020, my kids and I were at Strega, an Italian restaurant by the waterfront in Boston, planning to head over to my husband's cousin's house, and my son said, "Mom, I never told you this, but a week before Dad died, he called me and said, 'You know what, Michael? You don't have to play hockey anymore if you don't want to. I just wanted to let you know that, in case I'm not here.' It was just a weird conversation. I'd never heard Dad talk like that before."

To this day, I wonder what Michael meant. Was he thinking of committing suicide? Did he know that his habits would one day get him killed? He had been going down that dark road again, and the demons were coming out. I guess we'll never know.

Ally talks more about Michael than her brother does. "I miss him every day," she told me. "It's not like I only think of him once a year. I think about him all the time, and I wish he was here—just for another parent to ask questions, and I just would want him to be happy."

Then she asked, "Are you sad, Mom?"

"I'm sad as far as I miss talking to your dad," I answered truthfully. "But honestly, I miss him more like a friend."

"Yeah," she said. "I know that you and Daddy wouldn't be married today if he were still here. I don't want to hurt your feelings, Mom, but I don't think you ever really loved Dad. I mean, I think you loved him, but he was not the love of your life."

That was a lot to take in. My daughter was only fourteen when Michael was killed, but she already felt the struggles of her parents. I'm always saying to my children, "Communication is everything. That was one of the reasons my marriage didn't work." I know now that Michael and I kept everything too light. He never wanted to talk about how he was feeling or what was bothering him at work. Or at home. It was just hockey, hockey, hockey for him and skating, skating, skating for me. We were two people living in the same house, but we didn't share a life together.

"I don't want you to have a relationship like we had," I tell them. "Talk to your partner. Have something in common. Take an interest in the things they enjoy." The kids and I have a lot of difficult conversations nowadays. I never knew how important those were. We're all very different people than we were before October 19, 2014.

"You've done such a one-eighty, Mom," my daughter said to me recently. "When you used to take me to skating, everyone always thought you were the nicest person and stuff, but you were still very shy. Even if we went out with friends, you were just more intimidated and never confident in yourself. You're not the same person you were."

I still have flashbacks of going away on business trips with Michael, who often left me in hotel rooms by myself. He would come back a couple of hours later really mad at me. "You haven't met anybody? You're not mingling?"

"I don't know anybody here," I would argue. "You just left me. At least introduce me to somebody. And I don't know anything about the car business."

He used to get so angry, and then I used to get so angry because he never tried to understand how I was feeling. That was all it would have taken. A hand on my shoulder. Compassion. I realize now that those little things are what keep a relationship together.

It amazes me that now *I'm* the one out there mingling. I went to Las Vegas recently for a conference that dealers from all over the country attend. I knew no one. And of course, I was one of the few women there. A woman in a man's world. But a dealer from Rhode Island sat next to me on the flight. Someone I had met at a meeting a long time ago. We started chatting. "Maybe I'll see you later at the cocktail reception, and we can get together and talk more."

I said, "All right." And I meant it.

Our reception was at the Wynn, and I was running late in my high heels praying that I wouldn't fall. When I entered the ballroom, I couldn't find anybody I knew. That was when the usual panic began to set in. But I took a breath. I had been through too much at this point to be nervous. I had overcome so many problems. I knew my stuff. I was not little Suzanne anymore. I wasn't the girl who fainted at the first sight of blood.

I was going to be okay.

I spotted the dealer I had flown in with. "Suzanne, over here!" he called. "Sit down!" He was with his manager, and

I stayed with them for a while. And then I met a dealer from my 20 Group, and another guy, and another guy.

I thought to myself, *I'm good, you know?* It's still difficult. I don't think I'll ever be the social butterfly Michael was. But you know what? That's okay.

I'm me. The Suzanne who overcame a busload of people who wanted to see her fail, who had made it their mission to see her fail, and surprised even herself for being the last one standing.

For many years, I used to think there would have been no Suzanne if I hadn't married Michael Iovanna, the owner of Pride. But I'm starting to believe that I had it backward all this time and that there would be no Pride if Michael Iovanna hadn't married *me*.